Unravelled

Life as a Mother

MARIA HOUSDEN

Element
An Imprint of HarperCollins*Publishers*
77–85 Fulham Palace Road,
Hammersmith, London W6 8JB

The website address is: www.thorsonselement.com

 element ™

and *Element* are trademarks of
HarperCollins*Publishers* Ltd

First published by Element 2004

3

A catalogue record of this book
is available from the British Library

ISBN 0 00 718062 4

Printed and bound in Great Britain by
Clays Ltd, St Ives plc

In memory of my beloved father,
Ronald Guy Schlack

I have walked through many lives,
some of them my own,
and I am not who I was,
though, some principle of being
abides, from which I struggle
not to stray ...

'Live in the layers,
not on the litter.'
Though I lack the art
to decipher it,
no doubt the next chapter
in my book of transformations
is already written.
I am not done with my changes.

Stanley Kunitz, *'The Layers'*

Contents

Prologue

Summer 1975

"At the age of 12, I wrote the story of my life. The words flowed effortlessly onto the page; I knew everything then.

My sister Diana and I were leaning against the trunk of the maple tree that marked the dividing line between our backyard and the neighbour's next door. It was early August, a week before my 13th birthday; Diana was two years younger than me. We were bored and sweating in the heat, streaks of dirt creased into the backs of our knees and under our chins. I was wearing the same shorts and t-shirt I had worn the past few days and my canvas tennis shoes, which had been bright white at the beginning of the summer, were now scuffed and grey. Diana drew circles with a stick in the dirt and I waved half-heartedly at our younger sister and brother who were riding their bikes up and down the alley with a pack of neighbourhood kids, whooping and hollering each time they passed.

The two of us sat in the middle of a circle of limp white string that was tied to the wooden stakes our father had erected in an attempt to keep us off the grass he was trying to grow in the only shady part of the yard. Our father was nothing if not disciplined and persistent. Working long hours as a janitorial supply salesman during the week and as a member of the Air Force Reserves on weekends, his scant bit of free time was spent seeding and reseeding patches of dirt. Even so, our yard was mostly dusty sand, a constant parade of bicycles and endless games of 'kick the can' crushing any hope of lawn taking root.

Our house was one of the smallest on the block. It was painted grey on one side, white on the other. Years ago, someone had started painting it and never finished. My parents rented it from Mr Nyland, a stocky, good-humoured man who lived in a bigger house across the street with his wife and teenaged kids. Our neighbourhood was a mid-western mix of hard-working middle-class families and those who were significantly less hard working. The most scandalous thing to happen so far that year, besides the juvenile detention of the boy next door for 'borrowing' his aunt's car, was the impending divorce of my friend Anne's parents. Her father, a doctor, had been having an affair with one of his nurses. All the mothers in the neighbourhood spoke in hushed whispers about it. Nothing was said to us kids.

'I'm bored,' Diana said, flinging her stick across the yard.

I tipped my head back and squinted into the sun.

'Boring is what summer is,' I said. 'At least until we're grown-ups,' I added, thinking about our mother who was inside the house, stretched out on the couch in front of the fan, a cool washcloth folded neatly over her forehead. 'When we're grown-ups, we'll be able to do anything we want.'

'Yeah, as long as we don't die of boredom first. My butt's even falling asleep,' Diana said.

'Wait here,' I said, standing up and brushing off the back of my shorts. 'I have an idea.'

I was careful to be quiet as I let myself in the house. Mom didn't like us kids traipsing in and out, banging the bent screen door. I tiptoed upstairs to my dad's office, which was set up in the corner of my parent's bedroom, just down the hall from my brother's room and the one we three girls shared. I opened the bottom drawer of my dad's desk and lifted a stack of blank, white typing paper out of the folder in the back. I found two pencil stubs in the pencil holder my brother had made the previous Christmas out of an empty soup can and pieces of felt.

Diana was still sitting in the shady 'no man's land' when I returned.

'Here's what we're going to do,' I said, handing half the paper and a pencil to her. 'We're going to write letters to each other as if we're already grown up. You tell me about your life, and I'll tell you about mine.'

'How old should we be?' Diana asked, getting into the game.

'Oh, old enough to have everything we want, but not too old to enjoy it. You be 34 and I'll be 36,' I said.

I leaned back against the trunk of the tree and closed my eyes. The image of what I saw is as clear to me now as it was then.

Dear Diana,

My life is perfect. My husband James and I are happily married. We met when I was an architect just out of college, the year I published my first book. James is a wonderful man, a banker, tall and handsome with black curly hair, twinkling blue eyes and large, strong hands. We live on a horse ranch in the mountains outside Denver, Colorado, just the two of us with our 12 kids.

Our children are growing so fast. Justin, the oldest, is already 12. The twins, Elizabeth and Anastasia are 10, John is 9, Rebecca and Christian are 8, Emily is 7, Ben is 6, Julia and Molly are 4, Thomas is 3 and Sarah is 1. As you can imagine, they keep me very busy. I have time for myself too, though. I love to go horseback riding in the mountains, paint, write or play tennis during the day. At night, James and I often go to fancy restaurants with our friends.

Our family lives in a lovely old Victorian mansion that's painted blue with white gingerbread trim. It has a large porch that goes all the way around the house and bedrooms for each of our kids. A swing hangs from the branches of a tree in the front yard and in the back there's a playhouse with lace curtains in the windows, barns with chickens and goats, and a rolling, green horse pasture.

Despite the demands of our busy household, I am able to manage everything quite effortlessly. I love my life, and feel lucky to be the woman I am, the mother of 12 beautiful children, and James's wife.

I hope your life is wonderful too, and that you will be coming to visit us here soon.

love Maria

As I reread my letter before handing it over to my sister, I felt warm and quiet inside. I loved this woman I imagined I would become, this capable, vibrant, sexy, beautiful wife and mother. I knew that her toes were manicured, her purse well organized and her children well dressed and polite. I loved her life, the wholeness and fullness, joy and satisfaction in it.

I felt as if great things were possible for me, things that felt real and familiar even though there was no evidence of them in the life I was now living. I was a secret being kept hidden until the time was right, ripening and waiting for the external world to change before I could be revealed. Sitting beneath the maple tree in our backyard, I felt a deep quiet in the centre of myself as I imagined this woman I would become, as if it were already done, already true for me.

Each of us, in the most silent part of ourselves, has always known who we are. The eyes that look into ours from the image in the mirror recognize something that does not change with time or age. It would take me 24 more years to spiral into this centre of myself, to discover and begin living fully the sense of happiness and possibility that I dreamed for myself when I was 12. And, in the process, I would have to learn to be fiercely honest with myself and with others, and to unravel, with integrity and discernment, all my ideas about the way life is 'supposed to be'.

Ten Days, Ten Years

Summer 1998

Sunday

THE ONLY LIGHT IN THE ROOM CAME FROM A SINGLE KEROSENE lamp. I ran my hand along the wall beside the wide plank door, found a switch and flicked it on. A copper lamp with a fringed shade made a circle of light on the small wooden table next to the bed. I stood in the centre of the room and felt a sense of excitement growing in me. Although I had dreamed of this moment for years, envisioned this place many times before, I hadn't ever truly believed it would happen. Looking around now, I felt as if something new was coming alive in me, a sense without form, poised to take shape.

The idea of a retreat had been planted in my heart in the first months after Hannah's death. Holding her lifeless body in my arms, part of me had released itself; something in me had irreparably changed. I had known then that I would have to get away, to immerse myself in a silence that was only mine, if I were to ever understand fully what had happened, and to know what I was supposed to do next.

The Hermitage, the centre where I was now staying, had

been established years ago by an elderly Mennonite couple who had converted a huge barn into several floors of small bedrooms, libraries and a kitchen/dining room. For a modest fee, guests were given their own room and bath, and encouraged to spend their days quietly on their own, reading, painting, writing or walking in the fields and surrounding woods. All meals, except for breakfast, were prepared by Mary and served to guests around the farm table in silence. It seemed the perfect space for my retreat.

Now, gazing around the room, I felt as if I had been transported into another, timeless place, far from any life I had ever known. The walls were panelled with knotted pine boards that climbed horizontally to the beamed ceiling. Two screened windows on wide hinges were open to the warm summer evening, their white lace curtains catching the breeze. A well-worn plank floor was partially covered by a brown braid rug, and along one wall, facing the largest window, was a double bed with a carved wooden headboard and muted patchwork quilt. A small teddy bear with button eyes and suede paws leaned against the pillow.

I laid my suitcase on the bed and began to unpack. I stacked my folded clothes in the drawers of the simple bureau, placed my new journal alongside a silver pen on the desk that sat beneath the window across from the bed; I slid several photographs of Claude, and our four children, Will, aged 10, Hannah, who would have been 7, Margaret, aged 3, and Madelaine, aged 2, under the edges of the window frame. In the drawers of the desk, I put pages of drawing paper, a few pencils and a deck of cards.

Beneath the second window, next to the dresser, was a small kneeling bench with a wooden shelf nailed to the wall above it. Here, I placed a votive candle and the gold cross I wore around my neck during the last year of Hannah's life. When I had finished, I slid my suitcase under the bed, and sat down in the large, upholstered reading chair in the corner. From my vantage point, I could see fireflies blinking in the dark outside the windows. I sat quietly, not moving, feeling myself breathe, drinking it all in.

Mary had told me when I checked in that, apart from one other guest who was scheduled to arrive in a day or two, I would be on my own. Having shared a room with two younger sisters until I was 18, and never having lived on my own, the idea of such solitude and silence seemed too good to be true. As a wife and mother, I had become so accustomed to constant interruptions that I couldn't help thinking, in the quiet of the room, that this peace couldn't possibly last.

Sitting in the light of the flickering lamp, I heard a rustling noise just outside the window. I felt a shiver up my spine, feeling suddenly frightened of being alone, as if I might be smothered by the room's unfamiliar silence. Quickly, I stood up and with a running start leaped across the floor onto the bed, just as I had as a little girl, afraid of monsters that lurked in dark corners. Undressing beneath the covers, I dropped my clothes on the floor and burrowed beneath the soft sheets and thick quilt. Closing my eyes against the dark and silence, I fell almost immediately into a deep sleep.

Winter 1988

Slip, Sliding Away

My body was not my own; every pore was yawning open. Even the air particles felt charged with anticipation, poised for what was about to happen. The nurse, standing on one side of the bed, was anchoring my foot in the stirrup. Claude, his eyes wild with excitement, was holding one of my outstretched hands in his.

The whole of my life, 25 years, I had known this moment was coming with the same sense of certainty in which we draw our next breath. What I did not know was whether this baby, my first child, was going to be a boy or a girl. Claude and I had chosen to be surprised at the moment of our baby's birth. I felt grateful, in this breath between contractions, for the sense of excitement I felt, already loving this little person so wholly and completely without knowing for certain whether this baby was a Hannah or a Will.

The next contraction gripped my body, and all my attention was sucked into the sensation as I felt the weight in my pelvis bear down. I imagined the muscles around my cervix expanding and lengthening, the head of the baby, our baby, being pushed through. Dr

Menon, a petite Indian woman, smiled encouragingly from between my legs at the foot of the bed.

'You're doing great,' she murmured softly. 'Once this contraction subsides, I'll hold the mirror up so you can see the baby's head.'

I nodded briefly, consumed by the intensity of the crescendo running through my body as I tried to remember to breathe. Gradually, almost imperceptibly, the grip of the contraction released and my attention returned to what was happening in the room. Everyone got busy in the pause. The nurse helped the doctor position the mirror between my legs.

Claude asked, 'Do you want some more ice chips? Is there anything you need?'

'No, just keep holding my hand. I'm doing fine as long as I know you're there.'

I had barely exhaled the last word when the next contraction began. It rose like a tsunami from the centre of my body. Relentlessly, it rolled outward into the whole of my awareness, swallowing any separate sense of myself. I gave myself to it – opening, offering and surrendering. Leaning forward, aware of nothing but sensation, I saw in the mirror my swollen, bulging vagina, impossibly stretched around a protruding, dark orb. Dr Menon took my left hand and placed it gently on the wetness between my legs.

'That,' she whispered, 'is your baby's head.'

Some part of me, silently watching, suddenly woke up. As my fingers lightly caressed the slippery softness, the being whom until now had been an inherent part of my self and my body became in this moment its own separate person, touching me with its own, slippery head!

I took a deep breath and bore down again, feeling the burn of my perineum tearing. 'Breathe,' the nurse reminded me in a loud voice.

I pulled myself away from the centre of my body just long enough to expand my lungs and inhale another breath. I screwed up my face and bore down again. 'Relax your face!' the nurse spoke more loudly. I had never experienced such fullness in any moment; so many things were happening in my body and my awareness that it took everything I had to bring my attention to any single thing.

Then it happened. The intensely concentrated pressure pushing out from the centre of my body shifted slightly and began to slide. As the outer lips of my vagina became an expanding ring of fire around the baby's head, Dr Menon leaned in, closer to my body, and the nurse lifted the mirror out of the way.

'One more push, Maria. Make it a strong, good one,' she said.

Claude gripped my hand more tightly and turned his gaze from my face towards what was happening between my legs. I opened my mouth, inhaled a huge breath, closed my lips around it and bore down. I felt as if my body was being forced through my legs, outside of itself. For months, whenever I had tried to imagine the moment of my baby's birth, I always imagined my eyes closed as I concentrated on the last push. Now, instead, they remained fully open, allowing everything: the ring of fire, Claude's anxious face, the sweeping second hand of the clock behind Dr Menon's head, the relentless pushing, sliding, straining pressure inside me, between my legs.

Suddenly, the intensity popped, and I felt the baby's body, distinctly, easing through me.

'The head is out. Pant without pushing just for a moment.' Dr Menon and the nurse busied themselves with a blue-bulbed syringe, clearing the baby's mouth and throat. Claude started to cry, 'I can see our baby's face,' he said.

I could no longer contain the pressure building inside me. In a single rush, the rest of our baby's body slid into the world.

'It's a boy! It's a boy!' Claude exclaimed, tears rolling down his cheeks. The two of us couldn't take our eyes off our son's slippery form. Everyone, even the busiest nurse, was smiling. Although Will's umbilical cord was still attached to the unborn placenta inside my body, Dr Menon laid him, cheek to breast, against my chest. As I held our son in my arms, he gazed at me quietly, not crying, awake. Claude leaned over and kissed the top of Will's head, then turned to me. The two of us looked into each other, transparent and trembling as if we were seeing each other for the first time.

Dr Menon quietly interrupted our reverie by handing Claude a pair of scissors, instructing him where to make the cut in the umbilical cord. I stroked the top of Will's head and brushed my lips across his cheek. Instinctively, his head turned towards my breast. I slipped my nipple between his lips and he began to suck. I felt the goodness being pulled from inside me. As he nursed, Will's blue, deep-seeing eyes never left mine. For a single, timeless moment, the rest of the world vanished, and everything was my son and me.

Inheritance

Claude and I, giddy with happiness, were bringing our little boy home. As we wound through the quiet streets of our neighbourhood, I stared out the window and could not believe how much had changed in the two days since Will's birth. Everything familiar looked different and somehow more beautiful, as if the light falling on it had passed through a special filter, allowing it to be seen more perfectly and precisely than before.

Glancing at Claude's profile, I was filled with a sense that everything we had done together since we had married five years before had been in preparation for this. Each decision we had made, from finishing college to sending Claude to graduate school and saving enough money to buy our first home in a town with excellent schools, 45 minutes from Claude's parents, had been part of a carefully orchestrated plan. Although we had married young — I was 20 and Claude was 25 — each of us was sure that, like our parents, we would be married forever, and the two of us shared a sober determination to make an even better life for our children than the lives we had lived so far.

Feeling my eyes on him, Claude turned. 'I love you,' I said, blowing him a kiss. He smiled as we turned and pulled into the drive. Climbing out of the car, I gathered the diaper bag and small suitcase. Claude opened the door behind me, unhooked the safety latch and lifted Will in his infant carrier from the back seat. I followed the two of them as they passed through the gate of the white picket fence. The stone path led us past the rose garden. In early December, the bushes were mostly a tumble of bare branches, but the manicured lawn of the back yard was still a deep green. As we approached the back door of our little Cape Cod, Claude suddenly stopped and turned. Tipping Will's infant seat slightly forward, he said, solemnly but with a sparkle in his eye, 'Someday son, this will all be yours.'

The two of us had grinned at each other, drunk in our shared love for our son. Neither of us knew then, how far from reality our shared dreams were.

Uncharted Waters

Will had already crawled halfway up the steps when he turned, plopping his diapered bottom on the stair behind him, and giggled at me. Standing two steps below him, I smiled and clapped my hands encouragingly. I was trying to hide my concern, not wanting to scare him, half-wondering if I should whisk him up and away from danger, but feeling too excited to interrupt his climb. I couldn't wait to see the look on his face when he finally reached the top.

Will turned back to the task, and I slowly followed. As soon as he reached the top step, he scooted his chubby legs around until he was in a sitting position and, beaming at me, began clapping his hands. His delight in this new perspective, looking down on me, was worth every breathless moment I had experienced during his climb. I grinned and clapped too, reaching over to kiss his cheek.

'Good job, Will! You did it,' I said; I couldn't have been more proud than if he had just scaled Mount Everest. 'You must be so proud of yourself,' I said, reaching down to pick him up and carry him back down the stairs.

Two hours later, my friend Ann and I were sitting in her living room, which was comfortably cluttered with toys, unfolded laundry and half-drunk cups of coffee. Will and Ann's daughter Jillian were crawling around the gated, child-proofed space, mostly oblivious to each other. I admired Ann. She was the kind of woman I secretly wanted to be. Smart, sexy and sure of herself in a way that I wasn't, she was finishing her graduate degree in child psychology. She was unapologetically in love with Mark, her second husband, a talented and successful graphic artist, and the father of Jillian.

Ann seemed to know everything when it came to the health and safety of her child. I was sure she had memorized every dot and mole on Jillian's body while I, on the other hand, hadn't even remembered to count Will's fingers and toes in the moments after his birth. Ann seemed unconcerned about what other people might think about the way her house or life looked; as long as Jillian was happy, everything was okay. I was pretty sure my priorities weren't so noble or clear. I knew I loved Will as much as Ann loved Jillian, but I still considered the care and running of my home one of my primary responsibilities. It really mattered to me, the way things looked.

Every morning, after Claude left for work and Will went down for his morning nap, I scurried around, emptying and loading the dishwasher, dusting, vacuuming, making the beds and straightening each room. I had a list of daily, weekly and monthly household tasks taped to the refrigerator door, as well as a frequently updated grocery list, organized according to the supermarket aisles. I prided myself on my efficiency and organization, and loved it when Claude raved to friends and family about how quickly I had bounced back after Will's birth. Everything I did was done with one eye open to the way it would appear to someone else.

Now, listening to Ann with one ear, I watched Will practice pulling himself up to stand while Jillian crawled around on the living room floor. Ann suddenly paused in the middle of a sentence when she saw what Will was doing.

'Oh, my God! Look at him,' she exclaimed. 'He's going to be walking before you know it!'

I smiled, trying to look more modest than I felt. 'You won't believe what he did this morning,' I said, and then told her how he had crawled up the steps to the second floor. When I finished, I knew I was beaming, but I couldn't help it; I felt as proud as I had the moment he had reached the top. Ann, however, was more horrified than impressed.

'No! Where were you? Don't tell me you were there and let him do it. Now you're going to have to watch him like a hawk to keep him from doing it again,' Ann said.

The smile slid off my flushed cheeks as I took a sip of my tea to camouflage my embarrassment. Of course, Ann was right! What had possessed me to allow Will to do something so foolish and unsafe? Closing my eyes briefly, I vowed to be more attentive to my child's health and well-being. No matter how clean or well-organized my house was, it couldn't make up for the shame I now felt as a mother.

No Fooling

I bent down, placed my hands on either side of Will's face and kissed both of his cheeks. 'Remember, Muffin, Mommy always comes back,' I said.

'Yes, momma, I know,' he replied, throwing his arms around me for a final, quick hug before running to join the other two year-olds in his day-care class.

For the past year and a half, since Will was three months old, I had been working part-time as a financial analyst for a large telecommunications company. There had never been any question between Claude and me that I would return to my job after taking a maternity leave. After all, we both knew that I was a different kind of mother – more capable and independent than our mothers had been when we were growing up. Besides the fact that we could certainly use the additional income, it was important to me that Will, and any other children we might have, understood that while I was a wife and mother, I was also a woman, who had individual interests and a successful career too.

But lately, the last thing I wanted to do each morning was to pull on another pair of pantyhose, leave Will in the arms of someone else and pretend to care about a corporate job. Becoming a mother had rearranged my priorities in a way I had not expected. I couldn't tell if it was because I was unusually efficient or shamefully unmotivated that I now seemed to spend most of my time shuffling papers around on my desk, leaving file drawers haphazardly open, and making sure there was a complicated-looking spreadsheet on the screen of my computer in case a manager popped into my office unannounced. Stretching 10 hours of work into a 20-hour week seemed more exhausting than the actual work was.

Now, as I weaved in and out of the traffic, I no longer felt as certain about what I wanted as I had just a few months before. Rather than tailored suits and business meetings, a part of me longed for play dates with other moms and kids, turtleneck sweaters and jeans. It wasn't that I no longer wanted to be an independent, interesting woman or that I didn't value the idea of a career; it was simply that I couldn't help wondering if it might be possible to find a sense of meaning and usefulness in my life that wasn't connected to the amount of money I made or the work I did.

Monday

MY EYES WERE STILL CLOSED AS I LAY IN BED, INHALING THE cool morning breeze, feeling the weight of the quilt pulled up to my chin. I extended my arms and legs across the full length and width of the bed, savouring the spaciousness, knowing I could stay there as long as I wanted, listening to the cries of the birds greeting the arrival of the rising sun. Too excited to lie still for long, I opened my eyes and sat up, swinging my legs over the side of the bed. Through the curtains in the window, I could see golden fields of grass, stretching across rolling hills, to the faraway edges of trees.

I stood up and stretched my body. The silence in the room was as palpable as it had been the night before, but the light of morning had softened its effect on me. As I slipped on my robe and collected my soap and towel, I moved slowly so as not to disturb its spell. Everything seemed tinged with a kind of magic. Even the soap I had brought from home smelled sweeter than I remembered as I showered in the tiny bathroom across the hall.

Drying my body quickly, I pulled on a long cotton skirt

and t-shirt, and made my way barefoot down to the kitchen and dining room, one floor below. The night before Mary had showed me where to find freshly sliced bread, granola, yogurt and bowls of fruit. While the coffee brewed, I slathered two pieces of toast with homemade jam and peanut butter. Carefully balancing my breakfast on the tray, I climbed three flights of stairs to the top floor of the barn.

There, in a book-lined nook, I sat in a rocking chair in front of a triangular window, overlooking miles of fields, hills and trees. Sipping my coffee and nibbling toast while I rocked, I felt my body filling with a sense of exhilaration as I realized the whole day stretched before me, unscheduled. I could do anything I wanted, with no responsibility for anyone's needs but my own. Smiling, I felt my life, like the sun in my eyes, rising into a brand new sky.

As I lay on an old quilt in the shade of a maple tree, a tiny ladybug made her way across the page of my opened journal. Watching her slow, patient progress across what I imagined to be an unfamiliar expanse of white, I appreciated the simplicity of her journey – just a shell, some wings and a bit of determination. By comparison, mine and my children's journey, which had started in New Jersey three days before, had required the advance planning, packing and logistical consideration needed for a large-scale, military operation.

On the day we left, I had risen before dawn and loaded the minivan with suitcases, coolers of drinks and snacks, and several backpacks full of books and toys. It was a two-day journey from our home in New Jersey to where Will, Margaret and Madelaine would be staying with my sister and her family in Michigan, but we had packed enough supplies, games and activities to last us for four. After waking the children, I had fed them breakfast, helped them get dressed and then made sure each of them went to the bathroom before they climbed into the car. Claude had come downstairs to see us off, embracing each of the children, but barely looking at me. As I backed the minivan out of the drive, all three kids had waved to their dad and then shouted 'Ya-hoo!' in unison. The four of us could have been headed west in a covered wagon for all the excitement we felt.

Now, rolling over onto my back, I felt the matted comfort of the quilt under my bare legs and the soft cotton of the white eyelet pillowcase under my head. Lying in the cool shade, I caught glimpses of the afternoon sun as it danced between the spreading branches of the maple tree above. The colour of the ladybug's shell, the whisper of the maple leaves tossing in the breeze, the scent of crushed grass beneath my quilt – as I inhaled the sounds, colours and scents of life around me, part of me wished that my children were here to share the beauty and simplicity of the moment.

Yet, I also knew that it was only in being alone that I would have any hope of remembering everything I had almost forgotten.

It was late afternoon, and I was pacing around my room, feeling unhinged and restless. The residue of warmth and peace from my time under the maple tree had been tossed aside. My brow was wrinkled. My heart pounded inexplicably in my chest. I was out of breath but not tired, rested but not at peace. I couldn't help wondering if I had made a mistake in coming. After all, a voice whispered in my heart, what kind of mother would so willingly be separated from her young children for 10 days?

I could not shake off the feeling that something was coming, that I was here to meet someone. It was entirely possible, I reasoned, that my sense of loneliness and the pain of separation from my kids was causing me to wish for someone else to talk to, to reassure me. Either that or I was going slightly crazy in the unfamiliar solitude and silence.

I heard a phone ringing in the office downstairs. I raced to answer it, but the door to the office was locked. While I tried to figure out if there was a way to get in, the phone stopped ringing. Standing outside the door, I began to panic: what if it had been Claude trying to call me, or my sister Laura, or one of my kids? Although I knew they all had the phone number to my cell phone in case of an emergency, it didn't matter. The fear I was feeling now was not rational; it oozed like lava out of a dark place in my heart.

Plodding slowly up the stairs to my room, I began to cry. I felt helpless, impotent, disconnected from everything I had known as my life: my house, my family and my routine. Part of me felt frightened by the idea that Claude and my children could go on with their day-to-day lives without me. I missed my kids and longed to feel their arms wrapped around my neck, to inhale their sweetness, to listen to their voices telling me about their day. I felt guilty, physically sick inside, for having felt excited about being able to come here on my own, for choosing to spend time away from them.

Throwing myself on my bed, loud, hiccupping sobs began to pour out of my chest. My heart felt waterlogged, overwhelmed by a sense of loneliness. I wanted now, more than anything, to be able to take my children into my arms and apologize to them for every angry, frustrated word I had ever uttered. I knew that my family deserved to know the happier, grateful, joyful woman I had been in the shade of the tree, hours before, rather than the wife and mother I had been lately, an uptight, angry expression of my frustrations and fears.

Finally, exhausted from crying, I sat up in bed, wiped my nose and blotted tears from my cheeks. My eyes fell on the kneeling bench, along the wall, beneath the second window. I stood up and walked over to it, then slowly lowered my knees until they rested on the padded edge. Bowing my head, I closed my eyes and breathed. Gradually, as I allowed myself to rest there, I felt my heart begin to beat more slowly and a sense of calm filled me.

I became aware that even though my children and I were not in the same place, in some important way we shared the same heart. And my responsibility to them, to my family, was to use this time on my own to grow ever more appreciative and stronger. Then, and only then, I would be a better mother for having gone away.

Heart on a Limb

Claude and I were holding hands, our bare feet making side-by-side tracks in the white sand. Will, his bare bottom already tanned from days in the Florida sun, ran ahead, chasing sandpipers fanning across the beach in waves.

Weeks before, when Claude had asked me where I wanted to go on vacation, I had said, 'California' as I always did. We had both laughed when he replied, 'No, I've already been there. Let's go somewhere else,' because that was what he always said.

After having endured the shared pain and disappointment of two miscarriages in the past year, all the ways we were predictable together felt like a tremendous relief. It was also true that another baby was now alive and growing in me. This pregnancy, three and a half months along, seemed to have passed the critical point. I was finally coming closer to being the mother I had always wanted to be, now that we were making the leap from one child to two.

As Claude and I walked along, following Will, I savoured the feeling of my smaller hand in Claude's larger one. It was comforting to feel his presence, his strength beside me. Inhaling the salty air, I was aware of a deep sense of contentment rising in my bones, and I prayed that Claude was feeling it too. Losing the two pregnancies had catapulted each of us into a kind of isolated aloneness as we tried to cope with our disappointment and grief. At the same time, we had been brought closer together, feeling more determined than ever to create the larger family we both wanted.

Ahead of us, Will stopped short, turned, and began running full-speed towards Claude and me with arms outstretched. 'Mommy,' he said, wrapping his arms around my legs, 'I want to give our new baby a kiss.'

Claude and I smiled at each other as I bent down on one knee and lifted my shirt. Will leaned over, ran his small hands over the top of my bulging belly and gently gave it a kiss. As Will stood up, Claude reached down and swung him up into his arms.

'Hey, buddy, do you want a baby brother or a baby sister?' he asked.

'Oh, Daddy,' Will replied, 'I want a big brother, bigger than me!'

Poetry

I stumbled into Hannah's room, barely able to open my eyes as I made my way in the dark. My full, aching breasts had begun leaking down the front of my nightgown at the sound of her first cry. The light of the moon filtered softly through the blinds as I lifted Hannah out of the crib, settled into the rocking chair and she began to nurse. Leaning my head back, I closed my eyes and drifted off into some version of sleep. I felt a part of myself carried into the dark behind my eyes and lowered into a deep pool, while the rest of my body, although exhausted, stayed awake, aware of the soft weight of Hannah's diapered bottom in the palm of my hand.

I lost track of time and place as the two of us drifted there. Just as when she was inside my body only months before, it seemed as if there was no distinction between us. The only movement was my rocking and the back and forth sucking of Hannah's lips, the only sensation the tingly drawing down of the milk from deep inside my breast.

Eventually, Hannah's sucking began to slow and, not wanting her to fall asleep before finishing, I raised my head from the back of the chair and slipped a finger between her lips and my swollen nipple to break the suction. As I lifted her away from my breast, a few drops of milk spilled warm from her mouth onto my skin. I lightly kissed the top of her forehead, one, two, three times, and then lay her against my body again, guiding her mouth to my other nipple before she had a chance to protest. I smiled as her tiny fist closed around one of my fingers and she nuzzled closer and began to nurse.

As I gazed at her in the moonlight, at her long lashes lying against the translucent skin on her cheek, I felt myself drawn into a softer more primal awareness of the night. This silence, I knew, was the secret source of every mother's strength, a place where the quietest work of the universe happens, while the rest of the world sleeps.

Showdown with Robin Hood

It was a showdown between Robin Hood from the Dark Side and me, his mother. Will, now four years old, stood defiantly, hand on his hip, wearing a pair of green tights, a green felt cape and a red cowboy hat. A plastic bow hung like a necklace around his neck. In his other fist, he was gripping an arrow, jabbing it in my direction.

'Grrrrrrr …' he growled, his face scrunched into a fierce grimace, teeth clenched together.

I stayed where I was, three feet away. Crazy with fury – I had passed angry long ago – if he moved any closer, I thought, I might grab him, whack his bottom and stuff him in a closet. At that point I would have done anything to make him stop. Two hours before, I had been congratulating myself on having orchestrated a perfect day. How fast my fortune had changed.

Earlier that morning, I had woken before anyone else, washed my hair, put on make-up and packed the diaper bag. When the kids and Claude woke, I had unloaded the dishwasher and packed Claude's lunch, then spoon-fed Hannah in her high chair while Claude and Will ate breakfast. Later, after Claude left for work, I had dressed Hannah in new pink overalls and said a brief prayer of thanks when Will, without argument, agreed to wear a clean pair of jeans and a matching shirt.

Well-rested and organized with two perfectly groomed children in tow, I had arrived at Friday-morning playgroup promptly at 10 am. Sitting at my friend Karen's kitchen table, sipping coffee with the other mothers, I had breathed a quiet sigh of relief. Although being a mother felt the most natural thing to me, whenever I compared myself to others, I felt an anxiety that I wasn't doing it the way it was supposed to be done. I listened without comment while friends obsessed over their children's diets — whether foods were organic or contained too much sugar — too embarrassed to admit that I had, more than once, opened a bag of Oreo cookies at 9.00 in the morning simply to keep Will quiet in the car.

That wasn't the only secret I was harbouring.

Something was happening with Will. In the past few months, he had begun talking back and openly defying me, sometimes poking and pushing other kids. It was as if he were overdosing on testosterone. I had patience with him at first — my parents had spanked me when I was a child, and I had vowed not to revisit the same sin on my children. I was on a mission to create perfect children by being the perfectly loving, non-violent mother.

But, as the days and weeks wore on, Will's behaviour hadn't changed. In fact, it seemed to get worse. And so did I. I had started yelling, which initially appeared to shock him into listening. But then he got used to it and began to ignore me again. I had tried putting him in time-outs next, but when he refused to stay in one place, I would get angrier, grab him and roughly sit him on the edge of the bed. Finally, I began spanking him — not hard or often, but enough to feel ashamed and sorry later. I also made plenty of tearful apologies to him after, which only seemed to confuse him more. But I was at a loss at what to do, and it seemed that whenever I got aggressive and angry, Will's defiant, aggressive behaviour stopped. I desperately wanted to believe that Will's difficulties were temporary — a problem that I could nip in the bud before anyone else noticed.

I should have known better.

Thirty minutes into playgroup, before my second cup of coffee had cooled, a piercing wail rose from the playroom. Seven mothers, including me, shot out of their chairs. Even with Hannah in my arms, I managed to be one of the first on the scene. It wasn't pretty. As we burst into the room, Will, a plastic knight's breastplate strapped to his chest was standing over a bawling Eric, waving his arms triumphantly over his head.

Will turned to me. 'Eric was being mean to us!' he cried as I glared at him, trying to assess the damage.

I helped Eric to his feet and knelt in front of Will, my back to the others so they couldn't see my face.

'Tell Eric you're sorry,' I said to Will through clenched teeth. Eric was looking at his feet, wiping his nose with the sleeve of his shirt. The other three and four year-olds were standing in a circle, solemnly watching what was happening.

'No. He was the one being mean!' Will retorted, stomping his foot on the floor. 'Eric should say "sorry" to me.'

Just then, Hannah, who had been asleep in my arms, woke up and began screaming. Eric started crying again and ran to his mother. I felt the other women's eyes on me, imagining them, accusing and smug, outraged on behalf of their innocent ones. It was, I realized, a situation that could not be easily remedied. Deciding to cut my losses, I handed Hannah to Karen, picked Will up and carried him, kicking and thrashing, out to the car. Both kids screamed all the way home and anger swelled inside me. I was outraged at having had to abandon one of my few opportunities to spend time with people who didn't need me to help them to the potty. More than anything, though, I was furious with Will for 'outing' me as the bad mother I was.

Now, an hour and a half later, the two of us were facing off. Will was refusing to change out of his Robin Hood costume before going to the grocery store. As I stood there, I couldn't help wondering what had happened to the sweet little boy whose slippery form had slid out of my body three and a half years earlier, the baby who had slept on my chest every day in the warmth of the afternoon sun. In a little less than four years, I had managed to ruin the perfect little being who had been entrusted to me. I suddenly felt exhausted and my anger at Will vanished. Overwhelmed by my complete and utter failure as a mother, I sat down on the floor and began to cry.

As I wept helplessly, my face buried in my arm, I heard Will's footsteps approaching and then felt his arm slide around my neck.

'What's the matter, Mommy?' he asked, bending down to peek at me.

I lifted my head, wiping the tears from my cheeks.

'I'm sorry, Will.' I said. 'I just don't feel like a very good mommy right now.'

'Why?' he said, adjusting his cape to keep it from slipping over his shoulder. 'Is it because I want to be Robin Hood at the grocery store?'

In that moment, I saw something I had never seen in the same way before. As Will stood there, looking at me, waiting for my answer, I realized that he was a completely unique, intact human being in a little person's body entirely separate from me. Yes, he was dressed like a bad Western's version of Robin Hood, but what did that matter? I was dressed as a bad soap opera's version of a suburban housewife. Together, we made quite a pair.

I began to laugh and pulled Will into my arms. I understood then that I had been pouring so much energy into trying to make us and our lives look the way I thought they were supposed to look, that I was missing all the wonderful, unique things we already were. Just because I would never consider going to the grocery store dressed as Robin Hood, it didn't mean that Will couldn't. In fact, it was inevitable that there would be many, many more things that Will was going to like to do, to eat, to try, to be that I would have no interest in. His preferences for this or that had little or nothing to do with me.

And as for my frustrations with his behaviour earlier in the day, of course Will was going to have difficulties learning to get along with other kids, managing his angry feelings, deciding what he liked and what he didn't – at age 29, I was still struggling with the same things. But the important distinction I had not been able to make until this moment was that I was not Will's difficulty. My responsibility as a mother was to have compassion for Will, while at the same time trying my best to teach him skilful means of dealing with his feelings – and the situations he might find himself in. His behaviour, good or bad, belonged to him; what I did in response to it belonged to me.

Our differences and difficulties were not personal to each other; they were simply part of who we were. And the truest way I could express my love for Will would be to respect and celebrate both our connection as mother and son and our separateness as two, unique human beings.

'Come on, Will,' I said, holding his hand as I got to my feet. 'Let's go to the grocery store dressed exactly as we are. After all, even Robin Hood has to eat!'

First Steps

The mid-July sun was hot on our faces and shoulders, but the water along the stretch of isolated beach on Lake Superior had risen from the icy depths of the deepest of the Great Lakes, so our bare feet were red with cold. Hannah, 10 months old, asleep in the infant carrier strapped to Claude's back, had a yellow pacifier in her mouth and a rumpled white sun hat on her head. She had spent much of the morning pushing her stroller around our campsite, Claude and I cheering her on and congratulating each other that, like Will, she was going to be an early walker. I knew that anyone watching us would see that we were the perfect family, especially if they knew we also had a handsome young son.

My parents had invited Will to spend a week with them at the Cherry Festival in Traverse City, so Claude and I had decided to continue north after dropping Will off, and spend the week camping and hiking along the National Lakeshore. It felt great to have stepped away from the busyness of our daily lives. Now that we had become used to juggling the needs of two children, it felt easy to take care of just one. Almost a week before, we had pitched our tent on the sand, under a stand of pines, but although we had begun to feel more and more relaxed as the week progressed, the decision we had to make still hung in the air between us.

Claude and I were at a crossroads in our life. For too long, now, Claude had felt unhappy at work. The most progressive and experimental cellular technologies were being developed in companies on the east and west coasts, not in the midwest. As a design engineer, if Claude wanted to work with the best, we would have to move. But, to me, the thought of uprooting our family at this time in our lives didn't feel like such a good idea. In the past year, we had already experienced a number of significant changes. I had quit my part-time job soon after Hannah's birth, and although it was a dream we both shared that Claude would provide financially for our growing family so that I could be with the children at home, it seemed that neither of us felt happier or less frustrated, despite our new arrangement. The arguments between us had been growing louder and more hurtful, and more than once I had allowed myself to flirt with the idea of a divorce.

I couldn't help thinking of a story I had recently heard about Picasso. After sitting in front of Gertrude Stein for more than three months, painting her portrait, one day Picasso stood up and asked her to leave. 'I can't see you anymore when I look,' he said.

For some time now, I had felt as if I were experiencing the same thing. After eight and a half years of marriage, I felt more distant from Claude, rather than closer. Our love for our children was one thing we unquestionably shared, but no matter how much that meant to me, it did not feel enough. The life we had constellated together felt more like a fantasy than a reality, much less familiar and comfortable than either of us had expected it to. I was afraid that a move might leave us both feeling even more vulnerable, and further compromise the already frayed connection between us.

Now, though, watching Claude pick his way along the path ahead of me, moving carefully so as not to wake Hannah, the contrast between the glum, frustrated man who left the house each morning to go to a job he did not love, and the sun-tanned, smiling man ahead felt too great for me to ignore. This, I realized, was the adventuresome, curious man I had fallen in love with. Perhaps Claude was right – a change of life and scenery were exactly what we needed.

And, as his wife, it was up to me to support and encourage him to make the best decision for our family.

Running ahead to catch up, I grabbed Claude's hand and smiled at him as he turned. 'I think we should go for it,' I said. 'Your career is important, and you deserve to feel good about what you do. Besides, no matter where we move, with our kids and each other we'll be able to make any house a home.'

Claude's wide grin was the only response I needed. Throwing our arms around each other, I realized that Hannah wasn't the only one taking her first steps. I felt happy to have made such an important decision with Claude's interests at heart, and I couldn't help hoping that I was finally on my way to being the wife I had always wanted to be – the wife Claude had always wanted to have.

Shades of Gray

I waited in the silence of the examining room, listening to the sound of Claude's footsteps pacing outside the door. I breathed deeply into my lungs, trying to collect my thoughts and steel myself for what might come next. Despite the anxiety I felt, I was thankful that I had been able to think clearly enough to ask Claude not to come in. The terrified look in his red-rimmed eyes would make it difficult for anyone to believe the story I had decided to tell.

My thoughts were interrupted by a knock on the door.

'Come in,' I said as confidently as my voice would allow. The door opened silently and a white-coated doctor entered. I felt surprised and relieved to see that she was a woman, and then a flash of panic as I wondered if a woman might sense my fear more easily than a man.

'Hello, I'm Dr Martha Gray,' she said, advancing towards me, tucking her clipboard under her arm while extending her other hand. I felt my sense of panic rising as I became aware that my hands were shaking, and my heart was thumping in my chest. Dr Gray's expression didn't change. She shook my hand and then glanced briefly at the notes the nurse in the triage area had written on the piece of paper fastened beneath the board's clip.

'It says here that you sustained some sort of injury and now have blood in your urine.' She looked up from the clipboard, directly into my eyes. 'I need you to tell me exactly what happened.' The doctor's gaze was steady on me as I blinked twice, swallowed and then took a deep, shaking breath.

'I fell. I slipped and fell on the concrete steps outside our back door.' My voice sounded fine, stronger than I expected it to. I cleared

my throat again and continued more confidently. 'It was icy,' I explained. 'I caught the corner of the step as I fell, on the left side. I think the corner of the step bruised my left kidney.'

Dr Gray continued to look at me quietly. I couldn't tell from the look in her eyes whether she had believed me. I opened my mouth to say more and then closed it. I had said enough. She reached for her stethoscope and I willed my heartbeat to slow. I took a deep, shuddering breath. Dr Gray listened for a moment to my chest, and then gently raised my sweater to look at the left side of my back. Struggling to stay calm, I tried to erase the images in my head of what had happened in our family room less than an hour before.

Already, it seemed as if it were only a dream. I couldn't even remember what we had been arguing about. What I did remember was Claude ignoring me, his eyes staring straight ahead at the television, his lips pressed together, refusing to acknowledge me. I was yelling, begging him to answer me. Both of us had forgotten that Hannah was witnessing all of it, sitting halfway up on the carpeted steps.

Even if Dr Gray had asked me to tell the truth, I could not have remembered exactly how the moment had happened. All I saw was the image of me screaming into Claude's face, and him rising up from the couch, arms bent at the elbows, flailing. Somehow, his left elbow had slammed into the lower left side of my back. I could remember falling hard on the carpeted floor, and on my way down, seeing Hannah watching me, impassive, as if she were waiting.

I had lain there, for the longest moment. The next thing I recalled was that Claude had helped me up, and the two of us had stood, facing each other, eyes glazed over. Both of us were stunned. Becoming aware of Hannah, without speaking I had turned away from Claude *and started up the stairs. Picking Hannah up, I had carried her to her room and sat in the rocking chair with her, rocking and crying softly, apologizing over and over to her. Hannah had eventually fallen asleep. I had then put her in her crib and gone to the bathroom.*

It was at that point that I discovered my urine was pink. I went downstairs to tell Claude, who was sitting on the couch in the dark.

'There's blood in my urine,' I told him, woodenly. 'I think I should go to the emergency room.'

Looking now into the doctor's eyes, I held her gaze. I knew that the man waiting outside was not capable of the things these people might want to accuse him of. Telling the truth about what happened would only do more damage than good. Our heightened emotions, both good and bad, were undoubtedly due to the fact that in a little more than a week we were scheduled to move to our new home in New Jersey.

More than anything, though, I was certain that what had happened was not one person's fault or the other's. It was a warning to Claude and me that the problems between us were more serious than we had understood. And far from wanting to run away from them, I had seen today, in Claude's concerned, frightened eyes, a man I could love, a thoughtful man capable of caring for me.

Tuesday

I HELD THE BURNING MATCH CAREFULLY BETWEEN MY FINGERTIPS, and lit the three white votive candles on the altar. Sitting quietly on one of the straight-backed chairs arranged in a semi-circle in the barn's small chapel, I stared at the large wooden cross hanging from the ceiling and watched the sunrise through the stained glass window. The room was silent except for the occasional sputter of a candle flame and muffled footfalls from the floor above. Already, my third day there, I felt closer to God, not only as an idea but as a presence, a source of guidance that knew, even if I didn't, who I was and what I needed to do.

I was no longer alone in the barn. The night before, while Mary, Gene and I ate a dinner of homemade bread and warm stew, the sound of tyres on the gravel drive had interrupted the silence. The elderly couple had risen without speaking and gone outside to greet the visitor. I had heard the soft hum of voices, the opening and closing of a door, and footsteps on the stairs. Mary told me later, while the two of us washed the dinner dishes, that she had settled the new arrival, a writer, in a room on the barn's top floor. The four of us would be eating lunches and dinners together in the dining room, and the silence at meals would continue to be observed.

At the time, I had felt no curiosity about who the new arrival was. Now though, listening to the sounds from above, knowing that they were the footfalls of a writer, I began to wonder. I had always imagined myself a writer, ever since I was 12. But I had imagined myself many other things too, a pioneer woman, a painter, a world traveller, and I hadn't become any of those things either.

Watching the flames of the candles dance in the gusts of breeze coming in from an open window, I realized that all of those things, like the retreat I had once only imagined, were possibilities, opportunities to be something more, that only needed a breath of attention in order to come alive again. And if that were true, the first thing I wanted was the presence of this writer to inspire me to return to the book about Hannah's life and death that I had started, and then stopped writing, two years before.

A light, misty rain was falling, damping down the dusty road as I walked towards the mailbox, carrying a stack of postcards I had written to Claude, my sister and my kids. Although I was still missing Will, Margaret and Madelaine terribly, it was comforting to know that the three of them were together. I had grown up loving the fact that I had two younger sisters and a younger brother; I knew from own experience what company and fun siblings could be.

Despite the rain, dragonflies and bees continued to flit and buzz between flowers alongside the road, and ahead in the distance, streaks of sun pierced through patches of grey cloud. My hair was pulled back, caught in a large barrette and covered by a wide-brimmed straw hat. I was wearing a long cotton skirt and leather boots. Holding my head high, I was aware of the length of my stride and the swing of my arms. Smiling, I realized this was how I used to feel when I pretended to be a pioneer woman as a young girl.

Already, after only two nights on my own, I could feel my body unlearning its usual routine, reorienting itself to the track of the sun across the sky, to the rhythm and heat of the summer days. Reaching down, I slid a long blade of grass with its heavily seeded head from the stem of its root, rolled it between my finger and thumb, and inhaled its sweet scent. I felt a heightened sense of awareness, a deeper, more natural relationship with everything around me. Here, although I felt as far from my other life as I could possibly be, I felt much closer to the woman I'd always been.

Walking down the road, I glanced at the words on the postcards I had written to my kids and smiled when I imagined how glad they'd be to receive mail from me. Although I scarcely wanted to admit it, even to myself, I didn't feel the same way about Claude. I had written to him more from a sense of obligation than of joy. My sense of family, I now realized, was the image of me with my kids. And even though

Claude was my husband, my primary interest in him was his role as my children's father.

I stared ahead of me, into the expanse of the sky, and tried to remember if I had always felt this way. While there had certainly been times in our marriage when I could remember loving Claude as a man, not specifically as a father, lately it seemed our marriage was more about something we were working on than anything about love. For many years, Claude had been telling me he was unhappy with the woman and wife I was. And in trying to become the woman and wife Claude wanted, I had become a caricature of someone else's idea of myself. I had almost lost touch with the real me.

I also knew that it wasn't just Claude who was to blame for how far I had drifted. For as long as I could remember, I had believed that to be a good wife, I was supposed to change who I was. I also hated admitting when I was wrong, but hated even more being considered less than perfect by someone else. The quest to be a 'good' this or that was something I was all too familiar with. Now, though, I knew that I had to give myself the same permission to be imperfect that I had given Claude, and let go of trying to be someone I wasn't.

Reaching the end of the lane, where the dirt road met asphalt, I opened the mailbox and kissed each postcard before leaning it against the others inside. The last, Claude's, I held for a moment longer, wondering where my words would find him, and if, on reading them, he would sense the release of my grip.

Halfway through my lunch, I was watching the chickadees outside the window. After my walk to the mailbox and a late-morning nap in my room, I was filled with a palpable sense of connection with everything in my life, including the tiny birds I was watching, pecking at their seed, the sound of another's chair scraping across the wood floor, and the slightly bitter taste of rocket in my mouth. I didn't even glance up when the newcomer sat down in his place, where Mary and Gene had set it, directly across the table from mine. When I finally looked over at him, it was his clear–seeing blue eyes I noticed first.

He was a strong-looking man, about 50-years old, with a kind, laugh-lined face, large, long-fingered hands and silver-grey hair cropped short. He was smiling at me, in a familiar way, as if he were surprised to see me. We gazed into each other without words, filled with a sense of joy and delight. And although I had never met him before, in that single, timeless moment, I felt as if I knew the heart of this man and both my separateness and my connection to him. As surprised as a part of me was to feel such an unexpected rush of recognition, I knew, too, there was no need to try to do or say anything in response; he and I were the reason we were here.

I propped open the door to my room with a large field-stone and sat in the armchair, breathing deeply, my heart thumping in my chest. Even though the two of us, respecting the retreat centre's rule about silence at meal-times, had not yet exchanged a single word, I was hoping he would come.

Picking up my book and putting it down, too many times to count, my mind felt empty and yet too fully engaged to read. Finally, I heard footsteps descending the stairs, then coming louder and closer, rounding the corner. My body was thrumming with aliveness, my eyes looking for his when he stopped at the door of my room.

Seeing him, I instantly felt more sober than excited. The moment felt weighted with importance, and from the look on his face he felt the same way. Neither of us smiled as I gestured to him to come in. As he crossed over the threshold, I chose to remain seated, and studied him while his eyes scanned the room. He was wearing a white linen shirt, blue linen trousers and brown leather clogs. The part of me that was already writing a story between us was relieved to see that he was tall, almost the same height as me. Briefly, he sat on the edge of my bed, then changed his mind and stood.

'My name is Roger Housden,' he said finally. I caught my breath at the sound of his voice, momentarily disconcerted by his accent. 'I'm English,' he continued, 'a writer. Two weeks ago, I sold almost everything I had, moved out of the home I shared with a woman I lived with for 13 years, and came to America. I'm here on retreat, finishing my next book. Writing, I find, is solitary work. Because of that, and because I've just broken off with a woman I love, I intend to spend this next period of time on my own, thinking about what is next in my life. The last thing I'm looking for is to be involved in another relationship.'

I nodded, my mind trying to take in everything he had said without getting distracted by the conversations that were going on somewhere inside my head. From the first moment, I had known this man was unlike anyone I had ever known. But now, with only a little more information, the quietest part of me wanted to know more, while another felt so intimidated by our obvious differences, it wanted out.

'I'm Maria Martell,' I said, setting my insecurities aside and extending my hand. The strength and warmth of his grasp calmed me further. I gathered my courage and barrelled on. 'I was raised in Michigan, but now I and my family are living in New Jersey. I'm married. My husband, Claude, and I have been married for 15½ years. I've had four children,' I gestured towards the window where my photographs were hung. 'My daughter Hannah died of cancer four years ago at the age of three,' I paused, wanting to get this next part right. 'Although my marriage has been going through a rocky time, and I'm not sure yet what is going to happen, I believe that Claude and I are each other's best option. And if things don't work out between us, there is no way I want to get involved with anyone else for quite some time.'

I stopped, surprised and amazed that I had been able to be so concise and honest. Roger grinned. 'Well, then,' he said, 'It seems quite simple. I do have to say, I'm rather relieved.'

'Me too,' I said, smiling. I stood up as he moved toward the door, 'Thank you for coming, Roger.' I caught my breath, realizing how good it felt to have said his name out loud. 'I really appreciate things being clear between us.'

The two of us smiled and shook hands one more time.

'It was lovely to meet you, Maria,' Roger said quietly before turning and leaving the room. I felt my heart open and then close around the sound of my name on his lips. Shutting the door, I walked slowly to the window and stared at the photographs, as if through new eyes, knowing, as I did, the secrets beneath the smiles.

I was pacing back and forth in my room, feeling a strange combination of excitement and restlessness. Outside, the air, charged with anticipation, began to spill fat drops of rain that spattered against the windows. Then, as if on cue, there was a loud crack of thunder as a streak of lightning split the sky.

A freshly popped bag of popcorn filled my room with its buttery scent. I had carried it up from the kitchen a few minutes earlier, thinking I might take it up to Roger's room and offer to share it with him. But each time I headed towards the door, second thoughts stopped me in my tracks. Although I felt foolish for making a big deal out of such a simple thing – after all, it was only popcorn – sitting now on the edge of my bed, my heart was pounding as if I were about to do something wrong.

Closing my eyes, I felt like I might cry. I thought of other times in my life when I had talked myself out of doing something new, exciting or slightly dangerous, because I was afraid of what others might think or what I imagined might happen. I became aware that I had more regrets about things I had wanted to do but hadn't, than about things I had. I thought about the self-consciousness I had felt earlier in relation to Roger, and realized I was tired of being so careful, of feeling frightened, immature and small. The strong, confident woman I had been, walking to the mailbox today, would not be afraid to take chances in her life.

Gathering my courage, I picked up the bag of popcorn, and glanced at my image in the mirror. My cheeks were flushed with excitement, my eyes alive and clear. I felt a wave of elation rising as I pulled open the door and stepped into the hall.

A Colonial in the Suburbs

Claude was due home from work any minute and everything was ready. Will and Hannah were asleep in their beds, the table was set, and dinner was cooked and warming in the oven. Breathing a sigh of relief, I double-checked myself in the mirror, lit the candles in the centre of the table and put another log on the fire. Three months after settling into our new home in the suburbs of New Jersey, everything mattered more than it ever had. Claude and I had made a commitment to each other to begin this new life by making our marriage stronger, and I was more determined than ever to be the wife Claude needed me to be.

The incident in our family room in Ann Arbor had not done any permanent damage to my kidney but it had left both of us shaken and sober. Any problems we had experienced in our marriage up to that point paled in comparison to the violence we now realized we were capable of. Neither of us had yet pointed a finger of blame, in fact, we had barely discussed it. I knew the cause was much deeper than the specifics of that single incident, and I couldn't help feeling that speaking the horror aloud would only make it more real. What we had done was to schedule an emergency counselling session with the minister of our church and taken time out from our packing to return for another a few days later.

The minister had not seemed as alarmed as we both were. He suggested that as a couple we were under a great deal of strain, having experienced so many changes in our lives in the past year, not least of which was our impending move. He recommended that we make a point of spending more time together, putting the kids to bed early before the two of us ate dinner, and hiring a babysitter once a week so we could go out. Looking back, I remember the way Claude and I had held hands throughout the counselling sessions, too frightened to let go. Although the minister had not seen it, I suspect that our darker secrets, the real source of our problems, were buried beneath our fear of losing the only stability we knew.

Now, sitting on the sofa in the middle of the living room, waiting for Claude, I hoped this move was the new beginning we both needed. Claude now had a job he felt truly excited about, and we had been able to afford a beautiful house, a split-level colonial in the suburbs of New Jersey, bigger and more formal than the tiny Cape Cod in Ann Arbor we had grown used to. Fair Haven was affluent, family-oriented, and small enough that, until they reached high school, the kids could walk to school. Our house was just two blocks from McCarter Pond, where Canadian geese returned each spring to hatch and raise their goslings and neighbourhood kids went fishing in the summer and ice-skated in the winter. It seemed the picture-perfect place for the picture-perfect family we still wanted to be.

The headlights of a vehicle swept across the darkened living room. I stood up and looked out the front window in time to see Claude's car pulling into the drive. I glanced once more in the mirror and moistened my lips. Pasting a cheerful smile on my face, I waited for Claude to walk through the door. I wanted so desperately for things to work out between us, I refused to let myself think about the feeling I had, that I was standing in someone else's living room, in someone else's dream.

A New Life

I could hear Will, now five years old, and his friend Jeff giggling and teasing each other as they wrestled in the family room. Hannah was toddling around the kitchen, opening and closing the cupboard doors, while I unloaded the dishwasher and kept one eye on the casserole in the oven. It had been just over a year since we had moved to New Jersey, and I could hardly remember the life we had once lived in Ann Arbor. My days now were scheduled around Will's pre-school schedule and numerous after-school activities, and Hannah's play dates.

'Mom, me and Jeff want to go fishing at the pond,' Will shouted, as the two boys and their commotion careered up the stairs. 'Can you take us, please, please?'

I glanced around at the still messy kitchen, before turning to him.

'I'm sorry, buddy. I'm really busy,' I said. Jeff looked quickly down at his shoes, but Will could not disguise his disappointment.

'Please, Mom. You're always *busy,' he pleaded. I sighed, knowing it was true, but it wasn't easy keeping everything in order the way I liked it and Claude expected it to be. The recent memory of Claude standing in front of me, yelling 'I expect you to take PRIDE in this house. I want RESULTS! Trying is NOT enough!' still resonated in my head. I thought about the unfolded laundry piled in the middle of our bed, and the stacks of bills waiting to be paid.*

'I'm sorry, Will,' I said, truly meaning it. 'I really can't take you to the pond right now. I have too many things to do.' Tears started to well up in Will's eyes, as he slowly turned and motioned for Jeff to follow him back down the stairs. I felt as if a stone had lodged itself in my stomach, as I glumly wetted the sponge and began wiping the kitchen countertop. It was possible, I realized as I cleaned, that I

simply wasn't capable of being everything I needed to be. I couldn't manage to keep a tidy, efficiently run house, be an attentive, caring wife and a good mother. Even admitting the possibility filled me with a sense of relief.

'Okay,' I said to myself, out loud, 'If you can only do some things well, why not start with what matters most!'

Wiping my hands on the dishtowel, I took the half-cooked casserole out of the oven, and then lifted Hannah on to my hip. 'Come on, Missy,' I said, 'We have things to do. We're going for a walk to the pond to feed the ducks while Big Brother and Jeff go fishing.'

An hour later, I was sitting on a bench by the pond, lifting my face to catch the last rays of the afternoon sun. Hannah was digging in the dirt not far from me, while Will and Jeff patiently cast their lines into the water, occasionally catching and releasing small, whiskered catfish, but mostly reeling in clumps of slimy green seaweed. I loved the woman I was in this moment. Watching the sun dance across the water while listening to the happy chatter of the boys, I felt more relaxed, contented and patient than I had in a long time. I had already forgotten the unfinished tasks waiting for me, and willed myself not to think about whether or not Claude would accuse me of being lazy and undisciplined when he got home.

Staring past the far edge of the pond, I allowed myself only a whiff of a moment to imagine what it might be like if I were to start a new life with my children and no longer had to worry about what did and didn't work for Claude.

Wednesday

I CARRIED THE TRAY WITH MY BREAKFAST OF SLICED APPLES, coffee and toast up the stairs. Turning the corner, I noticed a small book leaning against the wall outside my door. I set the tray on the floor and picked up the book – it was a collection of poetry. I smiled, realizing it was from Roger.

The night before, although Roger had declined my offer of popcorn, he had invited me in. His room was a suite, with a living room, small kitchen and a bedroom loft. Stacks of books, dirty cups and glasses, and scribbled-on sheets of paper covered every flat surface. Roger quickly cleared a spot for me on the couch, and then offered me a cup of tea. I watched while he filled the kettle with cold water and lit the gas stove. Any nervousness between us evaporated in laughter, when Roger, having filled the teapot with hot water and Earl Grey tea, tried to cover it with a quilted toaster cover, having mistaken it for a tea cosy.

Sitting across from each other, me on the couch and him on a chair, I took a sip of the tea Roger had made. My face must have registered my surprise.

'I hope it tastes okay,' Roger said quickly. 'Being English, I automatically put milk in it.'

'It's good,' I said, truly meaning it, while suddenly feeling self-conscious and unsophisticated that microwave popcorn was the best I had come up with.

Soon, though, my flush of embarrassment was completely forgotten. Roger filled me in on more of the story of his life, and then listened attentively and asked many questions about me and mine. It was easy to speak with him, and I trusted the simplicity and openness between us. Our stories overlapped only in that he was married and divorced once and was the father to a 23-year-old son. Our age difference, he was 53 to my 36, felt less of a gap than the fact that he had lived all of his life in England, exploring, writing and taking photographs in exotic parts of the world such as Africa and India, while I, except for one ride over the Mexican border with Claude's parents, had never left the US.

Telling my story, seeing my own life in relief against his, afforded me a different perspective of all I had and had not done. I felt proud of what I had achieved and of what Claude and I had accomplished together. Being married, having children with a man I loved, and surviving Hannah's death were things that truly mattered to me. Rather than feeling I had missed out on a more exciting life, I realized that regardless of what I might or might not do in the months and years ahead, I felt proud and grateful for what I had experienced so far.

Just before midnight, as I stood up to leave, Roger reached for a book lying on top of a stack on his desk. Thumbing through its pages, he stopped, balanced his reading glasses on the end of his nose, and then read a poem, 'The Journey' by Mary Oliver, aloud. Now, standing in the middle of the hall, I flipped through the pages and read the same words again.

> *One day you finally knew*
> *what you had to do, and began, …*

Closing my eyes, I felt the same shudder of recognition I had felt the night before. I knew that newly discovered and yet unexpressed parts of myself were emerging, but I hadn't realized until now how strong and determined they were.

The rhythmic creak of the old porch swing and the scratch of my pen across the page kept me company as I rocked and filled my journal with my thoughts. Except for an occasional breeze, the air was mostly still and the sun made a dappled lawn of light on the forest floor. Pausing, my pen in mid-air, I watched a tiny brown mouse peek out from behind a log in the woodpile before scampering to the safe haven of an overturned tin bucket across the yard. Except for the fact that my kids were not there, I was surrounded by all the ingredients of a perfect day.

I had decided to spend the afternoon at Thoreau, one of the retreat centre's single-room cabins in the woods. The pioneer woman in me had always wanted to live, surrounded by trees, in a simple log home. Now, listening to the whispering leaves and feeling the integrity of an oak floor underfoot,

I could feel traces of that dream returning. Everything about this place felt comforting and familiar to me.

Standing up from the swing, I slid my pen into the binding of my journal and opened the cabin's screen door. Inside, a twin bed, covered with a yellow chenille bedspread, a pile of pillows and a folded patchwork quilt, was shoved lengthwise along the bottom of one window, serving both as bed and sofa. A wooden rocking chair with one spindle missing, a distressed pine table with a checked tablecloth and kerosene lamp, and a single ladder-backed chair were the only other furnishings in the room.

In one corner, wooden planks nailed to the wall held an assortment of mismatched plates, glasses, a bowl, a few utensils and assorted boxes of tea. Beneath the shelves stood a two-burner gas stove with a kettle on top, a simple plywood counter and a chipped porcelain sink. There was a well-worn broom leaning against the wall and a bottle of soap and a roll of paper towels. Judging by the cobwebs clinging to the ceiling and the pine needles on the floor, no one had seen a need to do much cleaning here for quite some time, and I saw no reason to disagree.

Unpacking my backpack, I set the table for lunch: a chunk of fresh bread, several slices of sharp cheddar cheese and a bright red tomato that I had picked on my way to the cabin as I passed the garden. While I ate, the water came to a boil in the kettle on the stove. A mug of chamomile tea perfectly complimented the soft, melted chocolate bar I'd brought for dessert. Washing the single plate and wiping the tablecloth clean, I thought about my other life, with its shelves of cookbooks, recipe card files and weekly menus, carefully planned and taped to the refrigerator door. I had almost forgotten how delicious a simple meal, much less a simpler life, could be.

The evening air was thick with the residue of the afternoon's heat as we made our way carefully along the path cut into the tall grass, me in front, Roger following. During dinner, the two of us had, with comical combinations of finger pointing and nods, mimed an agreement to take a walk together afterwards. I loved the fact that the most important scheduling decision I had made all day had been this single, spontaneous one.

Before leaving the barn, Roger wrapped a soft white silk scarf around my head to ward off mosquitoes. I buried my nose in it, inhaling a musky cinnamon scent. Smiling, he said, 'I knew it would look beautiful on you. I brought it back with me from India.' He continued, 'If you don't mind, I have what might sound like a strange request. I'd like to share this walk with you in silence.'

Returning his smile, I agreed.

Now, wearing the scarf, picking my way into the twilight of the day, I felt grateful for the quiet. Although I had always loved the experience of silence when I was on my own, this was the first time I could remember, outside of church, that the silence between me and someone else was intentional rather than uncomfortable. It felt more like a fullness than an absence and allowed me to observe how my mind kept coming up with things it wanted me to tell Roger. I had not realized how much of my interaction with other people was social rather than real. This explained why I came away from so many conversations feeling exhausted and empty; in truth, nothing much had been said.

Cresting one of the taller hills, the two of us paused and turned. Below, the retreat centre's grey weathered barn was the tiniest dark shadow of a ship in an ocean of waving, yellow grass. We stood together, watching the shadows deepen as the last of the light faded from the landscape. Finally, turning, Roger took the lead as we began the long walk back to the barn.

I followed slowly, feeling like a woman from some exotic place. I imagined myself on one of Roger's journeys, walking in silence through the Sahara desert in the tracks of the Bedouins and their camels. It was as though a part of me already knew what it was like to lay on the sand, watching the moon rise into an African night sky, covered by a nomad's wool blanket.

As we neared the barn, Roger stopped in the middle of the path. The two of us stood, not speaking, our chins raised towards the stars. I smiled, appreciating how unexpectedly familiar everything in this moment felt. Although I was not facing him, I felt the shift in Roger's gaze as his eyes began to seek my face. Turning, I felt a question, without thought, completely unbidden, rise out of my heart.

'Haven't you recognized me yet?' I asked.

Dark Side of the Moon

Hannah was lying in the hospital bed, sleeping peacefully for the first time in days. The painkillers, coursing through the IV line into a vein in her left arm made sure of that. Claude and I, our eyes red from too much crying and not enough sleep, sat in chairs on either side of the bed, staring blankly at each other and her. Although I could trace every moment back from this one, I still couldn't believe we were here. It was as if we had moved into another dimension of reality no one would willingly enter. Claude and I hadn't yet had time to allow what was happening to sink in, but we knew from the faces of the doctors and nurses who had already spoken to us, that whatever was happening with Hannah, it wasn't good.

The door opened, and one of the doctors – Hannah's pediatrician Dr Edman – motioned for us to join him in the hall. I glanced quickly at Hannah before standing, wanting to make sure she wasn't going to wake up and panic when she realized we were gone. She looked so tiny in the middle of the hospital bed, her skin translucent in the half-light. Kissing her lightly on the cheek, I whispered, 'Daddy and I will be just outside in the hall.' She didn't even stir.

Standing up and following Claude and Dr Edman out of the room, I felt unsteady on my feet, but strong and determined inside. Whatever was wrong with Hannah, I knew we would do whatever needed to be done to fix it. Looking at Claude in the glaring light of the hospital corridor, he seemed less certain. His eyes kept darting from the doctor's face, to mine and then to the busy nurses who were readying carts for the morning rounds of medications.

Dr Edman led us into an empty room next door to Hannah's. He perched on the edge of the bed, leaving the chairs for Claude and me. We sat down and I inched my chair closer to Claude's and reached out to hold his hand. Any animosity or distance between us had disappeared since we'd brought Hannah into the emergency room with blood in her urine the day before. The possibility that Hannah might be seriously ill had catapulted us beyond our own small concerns.

Dr Edman cleared his throat and looked steadily from Claude to me. 'The x-rays we took yesterday confirmed that there is a mass in Hannah's abdomen. We can't know much more than that until we do a biopsy. I'm going to schedule her for emergency surgery this week. Hopefully, the surgeon will be able to remove the whole tumour. Even if he can't, we'll be able to send a piece of it to the lab and then we'll know more.'

A tumour — it was a word I knew, but I never imagined it was something that could grow inside an almost three-year old girl, much less my own daughter. I searched Dr Edman's eyes, looking for clues to what it might mean. I didn't want to ask the question that rose up in my mind at the sound of the word, but I couldn't stop myself.

'Does a tumour mean cancer?' I asked. Claude swung around to face me and, although I was still looking at Dr Edman, I caught a glimpse of the horror in his eyes. I was not sure if he was angry with me for having spoken the dreaded word out loud, or if he was stunned because he hadn't yet thought of the possibility. Either way, it didn't matter. I had to know what we were dealing with, so I would know how best to help Hannah.

Dr Edman didn't answer right away. I imagined he was searching for the right words. Finally he spoke. 'A tumour doesn't necessarily mean cancer,' he began, 'but in this case, it very likely is. We know it has grown significantly in a short period of time. As you told us, when you took her to the emergency room in Michigan a few weeks ago while you were on vacation and Hannah was complaining that her stomach hurt, the doctors there could find nothing wrong. This tumour, as it is now, is about the size of a small soccer ball. If it was the same three weeks ago, the doctors couldn't have missed it.'

Dr Edman's voice was steady and measured, and I felt myself wanting to resonate with his calm. I knew I needed to think more clearly than ever before, to be able to consider carefully what needed to be done, despite the clamouring voices in my head. I had so many questions, but I also understood what Dr Edman was telling us – that they couldn't know anything of substance until they had opened Hannah up. Suddenly, the image of Hannah sedated on an operating table came into my mind and I began to shake. Claude squeezed my hand and laid his arm across my shoulder. I leaned into him and immediately felt my sense of balance returning. Claude took a breath, and then spoke.

'Can you tell us why they might not be able to take the tumour out?' he asked.

'Well,' Dr Edman responded, 'There's a chance, because it's so large, that it may have infiltrated one or more of the surrounding organs. We already know that we're going to have to remove at least all or part of one organ. The tumour seems to have grown out of Hannah's left kidney.'

A bomb exploded in my gut. I felt Claude's body contract as if he was going to double over and throw up. I closed my eyes, desperate to wake up from the hell realm, but all I could see was the image of my body, crumpled on the family room floor, and Hannah, on the stairs, watching. It was as if I, looking through a wide-angle lens, had been afforded an even more terrible perspective on the thread connecting *the story of our lives. It was only a little more than a year before that I had gone to the emergency room with blood in my urine from an injury to my left kidney.*

Daddy's Girl

Hannah was sitting on my lap in her wheelchair, playing with my hair and kissing my cheeks. I stared into her eyes, wanting to absorb the love and tenderness I saw there. She was hooked up to an IV pole, which she was now able to manoeuvre deftly, as it followed her like a shadow wherever she went. Her head was mostly bald, except for a few wisps of blond hair, and her body was thin and weak, side effects from the chemotherapy drugs she had been receiving as part of the bone marrow transplant procedure. The two of us had been living in the hospital for more than a month, mostly in isolation, on the paediatric oncology floor. We both felt a sense of elation now that her immune system had recovered sufficiently enough for her to be able to come out of her room.

It had been five months since Hannah was officially diagnosed with a rhabdoid tumour of the kidney. The doctors were honest with us that the chances of survival beyond 15 months were slim. Even so, treatment was begun immediately, and when she relapsed less than two months later, we agreed to the bone marrow transplant. Claude and I insisted that Hannah be allowed to attend pre-school gymnastics class, and participate as a three-year old in life as much as she was willing and able.

For her part, Hannah was an inspiration to everyone around her. Quickly acclimatizing to life in the hospital, she demanded that doctors and nurses introduce themselves to her using their 'real' first names, and became known as the 'little girl with the red shoes' because she insisted on wearing her new, red patent leather Mary Jane's everywhere, even to surgery. The reason we were both sitting in the same wheelchair now was that Hannah had asked if the nurses would bring a 'grown-up' chair large enough to hold us both so she could ride to her MRI sitting on her mommy's lap.

Now, as we waited for the nurse to escort us into the darkened room where the MRI machine was, I prayed that Claude would arrive in time. He had promised Hannah on the phone that he'd leave work early and make the long drive to the hospital to ride into the machine with her. But I knew that the project he was working on was months overdue, and Claude's manager and team members were relying heavily on his expertise.

It had helped that his parents had come from Michigan to be with Will and take care of the house for the six weeks Hannah and I were away, but even so, Claude was under a lot of pressure from all sides, and I couldn't help wondering how long he could go on. I also knew that none of this would mean anything to Hannah, as the MRI was the test that frightened her the most. She understood that while I could watch what was happening from the control room, because I was already several months pregnant, I could not go in the machine with her.

The news of my pregnancy had been received with amazement by most of the people in our lives, but Claude, Will, Hannah and I couldn't have been more thrilled. Far from accidental, Claude and I had wanted this baby. Watching Hannah's sedated body being wheeled into her first surgery, we had clung to each other, in the semi-privacy of a curtained alcove in the waiting room, knowing without question that whatever the problems between us, our children mattered more to us than anything else – and we wanted, needed, to have more. Three months later, my pregnancy test came back positive, and we shared the joyous news with a beaming Will and Hannah on Christmas Day.

Now, without wanting to alarm Hannah, I couldn't help glancing from time to time towards the door at the end of the corridor. Hannah stroked my worried face with her small hands: 'Don't worry, mommy. Daddy will come. He told me. I know.'

I smiled, looking into her eyes, and prayed that she was right. Just then, the door at the end of the hall opened and Claude came striding through. Hannah turned and shrieked, 'Daddy', extending her arms towards him. Claude, grinning from ear to ear, broke into a trot. Reaching us, he scooped up Hannah gently off my lap and buried his face in her neck.

'I knew you would come, Daddy,' Hannah said. Claude looked over Hannah's shoulder at me. We both had tears in our eyes.

'I love you Missy Hannah,' he said, his voice choked with emotion. 'Nothing could stop me from being with you here.'

I smile at him, grateful and relieved. Bending down, with Hannah still in his arms, Claude gave me a kiss.

'How are you feeling? How's our baby doing?' he asked. I placed my hand on my stomach.

'I'm a little tired, but everything seems great,' I said. Claude smiled, and nodded.

The door to the MRI room opened, and a nurse motioned in our direction. I stood up from the wheelchair and pushed Hannah's IV pole behind Claude, who carried her. We had been here before, so I knew to expect the darkened room with its single, soft light above the control panel. The technician held the door to the MRI machine room open, and I watched Claude and Hannah through the glass window as they went in. Gently, Claude laid Hannah on her back on the narrow board, while the technician wrapped Velcro straps around Hannah's head, arms and legs to keep her still.

As soon as she was in place, Claude folded his 6 ft 6 in frame almost in half, and lay on his side on the same narrow board, just below Hannah's feet. I caught my breath and tried not to cry as I watched Hannah move one of her hands slightly so her fingers could touch the top of Claude's head. The technician double-checked everything, then joined me in the control room, closing the door behind him. As he flicked a series of switches, a huge roar began in the next room. As the magnetic drums inside the machine started to rotate, the platform Hannah and Claude were on slowly slid into the darkened chamber.

It seemed like hours, although I knew it was only minutes, that Hannah and Claude lay in the centre of that terrifying roar. Although a part of me wanted to close my eyes, I knew that moments like this mattered in a way that so many others didn't. If I could imprint this image on my heart, I would never forget what Claude and I, together and separately, were willing to do for love.

Seen and Unseen

The organist was playing the last bars of the opening hymn, when the four of us entered the church and made our way quickly down the aisle. Claude, handsome in a suit and tie, carried Hannah in his arms, while Will and I, holding hands, followed closely behind.

Despite her illness, Hannah looked beautiful. She was wearing her favourite Easter dress, with a white lace headband wrapped around her almost bald head, and her red patent leather shoes. Looking over her dad's shoulder, Hannah smiled and waved at Will and me. I smiled back, knowing I looked about as good as I could in my silk maternity dress, cheeks flushed with make-up and pregnancy's glow. Will glanced up at me, and I winked at him and squeezed his hand. He looked handsome, older than his six years in khaki trousers, blue sport coat and tie, and yet I was also aware of how small his fingers felt wrapped around mine.

Filing into an empty pew near the front of the sanctuary, the four of us sat down, Claude and I anchoring each end with Will and Hannah in between. Digging into my purse, I pulled out two boxes of raisins, a few blank pieces of paper and a bag of crayons.

'You're such a good mother, always so well-prepared,' the woman behind me whispered in my ear. 'It's a real treat to see such a nice family with children that are so well-behaved.'

I turned and smiled, grateful for the compliment, but wondering what the woman might have said if she had been a fly on the wall in our house that morning, listening to Claude and me bickering back and forth, yelling at our kids to get ready for church. I could never have imagined, before Hannah got sick, that life could return so quickly to normal. Within weeks of Hannah's and my return home from the hospital, our family had slipped into a more regular routine, which included the less than stellar dynamics between Claude and me. It was now clear that in the face of a crisis, Claude and I were capable of being on our best behaviour, but as soon as the crisis was temporarily averted, the residue of resentment between us floated again to the surface.

Now, settling back into the pew, inhaling the sense of peace I always felt in the church's silence, I couldn't help wondering which was more true – the story of us sitting here, all together, the perfect family at church on Sunday morning, or the frustrated, angry life and lies that nobody else could see?

Eating the Sun

Hannah didn't look nearly as sick as the doctors said she was as she arranged the Oreo cookies in two stacks on the plate in front of her. In the months since her bone marrow transplant, her hair had grown back, short and downy soft, her cheeks had become rounder and pink, and her strength had returned. This morning, on waking, she had clambered up the steps to our room and jumped in between Claude and I in bed, exclaiming, 'Mommy, I have the very, very best idea. Can me and Will have Oreo cookies for breakfast?'

Her eyes were so bright and mischievous, both Claude and I laughed out loud, and with barely a second thought I had said, 'Yes.'

A month before, doctors had discovered another tumour in Hannah's abdomen. This time it was inoperable. The only treatment options available were highly experimental and would require Hannah to spend every day of what remained of her life in the hospital, with no guarantee of remission. Claude and I were sick with despair but were in agreement about what was best for Hannah; with leaden hearts we had told Hannah's doctors we were taking Hannah home and would not subject her to any further treatment.

Claude had continued to pray every night for a miracle, as he had ever since Hannah's diagnosis. And while I held my heart open to every possibility, I also felt that the best I could offer Will, Hannah and our family was my willingness to be both honest and practical about what needed to be done next. No one could tell us exactly how much longer Hannah would survive, whether she would be able to hold our new baby, due in three months, or to celebrate her fourth birthday, which was four months away. Her doctors had said any estimate they could give was at best a guess.

We had broken the news to Will and Hannah as gently as possible, telling them that the lump in Hannah's tummy had returned and this time the doctors couldn't take it out. Although many people had disagreed with our decision to be honest with our children about what was happening, we both felt strongly that Will and Hannah deserved an opportunity to hear the truth from us, rather than trying to guess what was happening or to overhear it from someone else.

But even I was unprepared for their reactions. Will hugged me and then hugged Hannah, thanking me over and over that, because he knew Hannah was going to die, he could now make a point of being especially nice to her every day she was alive. Hannah, in her own extraordinary way, immediately announced that she was going to heaven to be with God and his angels, and that what she wanted more than anything was to be able to see her new baby sister or brother and to die at home, in the bed that smelled like her mom and dad.

Now, as I puttered around the kitchen and listened to Will and Hannah's happy chatter, I felt grateful we had agreed to the cookies-for-breakfast diet. As I poured a second glass of milk for each of them, I heard the doorbell ring downstairs. I called down, 'Come in, the door's open,' and smiled when I saw it was Rhea, Jeff's mom, and Jacqueline, Jeff's little sister, who was the same age as Hannah and one of her best friends. The two of them came up the steps into the kitchen, and when they saw the chocolaty happiness on Will and Hannah's faces, Jacqueline's eyes lit up, although Rhea didn't look too sure.

'We're having cookies for breakfast,' Hannah announced proudly. 'Do you want some, Jackie?' she asked, holding several cookies in her hand, gesturing for Jacqueline to take them. Jacqueline turned to her mother.

'Can I, please Mom?' she pleaded.

'I don't know. Cookies for breakfast?' Rhea asked, looking at me.

For a moment, I wondered if I had goofed again as a mother. For months, several people – one of them a very close friend of mine – had suggested it was irresponsible of me not to put Hannah on an all-organic, macrobiotic diet. At the time, while I had agreed that for some people with cancer it might be the right decision, I had felt that Hannah was too young to be subjected to such a rigorous regime, especially since eating was one of the few pleasures that remained for her. Now, though, the part of me that had always wanted to believe there was something we could do to save Hannah, was saying, 'I told you so' and poking me in the ribs.

Hannah, perhaps sensing my uncertainty, let out a loud guffaw. 'What's the big deal?' she laughed, handing the stack of cookies to Jacqueline. 'They're just cookies. Go ahead, it's okay.'

It was like one of those moments in the movies, when the clouds part and the light shines through. They were just cookies, but this wasn't just any day. This was a day when Hannah was happy and sick, when she and her brother were loving each other and covered in chocolate. I knew that we needed to inhale these miraculous, joyful moments with Hannah, the way plants eat the sun all summer in order to survive the long, winter months ahead.

Thursday

My face was close enough to the freshly mown grass to inhale its sweet scent and notice that the blades not yet touched by the morning sun were still strung with pearls of dew. I woke early, and after a small breakfast and a half hour of prayer in the chapel, I packed my journal, an orange, two granola bars and a bottle of water in a paper sack, rolled my quilt into a manageable roll, and carried it all along a path to a circle of cut grass on the crown of one of the hills.

Lying on my stomach, my chin in my hands, I watched birds dart in and out of the grass, chasing insects with iridescent wings. Below, a farmer and his tractor made back and forth furrows, while above, white ribbons trailed silvery airplanes across the bowl of blue sky. I forgot all about my journal and the things I had come there to think about, and instead, laying my head in the crook of my arm, concentrated on the warmth of the morning sun on the backs of my legs and tried to notice everything I might not otherwise have seen.

I had not even realized I was asleep when, drifting up, I felt myself drawn into consciousness by the presence of another.

Keeping my eyes closed and careful not to be distracted by the sounds of crickets and buzzing insects in the grass, I allowed myself to float in the darkness behind my eyes until the image of a woman gradually emerged.

She was standing with her arms outstretched, beckoning me. Tall, like me, but older by about 30 years, she was beautiful in the way that a woman with confidence is, her gaze strong and tender at the same time. Her face wore the lines of one who has loved deeply and is still loved, of one who has known pain and grief without running from either. I could feel that she was stronger than me – and more graceful too – willing not to have all the answers. I knew, in a way you can only know in dreams, that this woman liked to write and paint, that she enjoyed her work and that now, although her home was often filled with the laughter and voices of family and friends, except for her big dog, she lived mostly on her own.

Moving towards her embrace, I felt curiously at peace. As she wrapped her strong, vital arms around me, she said quietly in my ear, 'It's okay, honey, don't worry, it's going to be alright.'

As soon as I heard her voice, I knew. This woman, who was holding me in her arms with so much understanding and compassion, was the woman I was going to become. Everything I was going to be, this woman already was. She loved me, cared for me and was able to look at me with such unconditional regard because she had been me, had been where I was now. I realized, then, just as I had in the first moment of meeting Roger, that at some level I wasn't going to have to figure out whether to do this or that in my life. Everything that needed to happen would happen, and everything that needed to be done would be done.

I was sitting at the desk in my room, holding a pen in my hand, staring out of the window. I had returned from my nap on the hill too late for lunch, but Mary had left a plate of sliced cucumber, bran muffins and a scoop of fresh corn and pepper salad in the refrigerator for me. The plate lay empty on the desk beside me now, the meal already forgotten as I searched for words to describe the feeling of the dream I'd had of the woman I was going to become.

It felt necessary, important somehow, to allow moments like this to re-filter through me so that I might capture the essence of their offerings and articulate them on the pages of my journal. These days an almost constant stream of memories was pouring through me, and powerful images and realizations were coming to me in dreams. I was beginning to understand that perspective was one of the things that had been missing in my life. I suspected that in the future I would need to remind myself again and again of the lessons I was learning now.

Suddenly, a steady, piercing tone cut the air. I knew instantly it was a fire alarm! I jumped up, aware that I should head straight outside, but instead I turned the corner in the hall and raced up the stairs towards where the sound of the alarm was coming from. Out of breath, I stopped in the centre of the upstairs hall. Smoke was pouring from a crack in the door of Roger's room.

'Roger,' I shouted, surprising myself with the level of panic in my voice. Bursting through the door, I almost ran into Roger who was standing in the middle of the living room, waving a dishcloth in each hand. A burnt black bagel lay on the kitchen counter.

'I was trying to toast it over the burner on the gas stove,' Roger explained sheepishly. 'Then I got involved in my writing and forgot.'

I took a deep breath and felt my chest swell with relief. Roger looked so helpless standing there, bare-chested, in running shorts, two faded dishtowels in his hands, that I couldn't help laughing.

'Oh my God, in a barn made of wood! I was sure we were goners!' I said, finally.

'What a disaster,' Roger said, laughing now too. As I stood on my tiptoes to remove the battery from the droning smoke detector, he opened all the windows and fanned the smoke out of the room. Finally, when we were finished, he turned to me.

'If you'd like some,' he said, still smiling, 'I think I could manage, without too much problem, to make us some coffee.'

'Yes, that would be lovely,' I said.

I watched while he pulled the coffee maker towards him, dumped an unmeasured portion of coffee in the filter, and then poured an equally unmeasured amount of water from the kettle on the stove into the machine.

'Shouldn't you pay attention to how much coffee and water you're using?' I asked, as diplomatically as I could.

Roger turned away from what he was doing to look at me and, seeing the concerned look on my face, grinned.

'I never measure anything,' he said, his eyes dancing, 'That way, it's always a surprise!'

I felt a door open unexpectedly in me. There was no way, I would ever have thought of it that way. While he continued to busy himself in the kitchen, I excused myself to go to the bathroom. Washing my hands, I noticed his black leather shaving bag on the counter next to the sink. I hesitated only a moment before taking a peek: a well-worn toothbrush, toothpaste, a tube of Dr Kiel's moisturizing lotion, a tiny bottle of tea rose oil, Body Shop deodorant and Eternity, a Calvin Klein cologne.

Returning to the living room, I made room for both of us on the couch, while Roger carefully carried two mugs of coffee from the kitchen. As he handed me mine, our fingers brushed past each other and I felt a rush of energy, like electricity, run up my arm. It was so unexpected, that I instantly felt self-conscious and bent my head quickly to take a sip. Roger sat down, and although no part of our bodies was touching, there remained a palpable energy, like warmth, jumping back and forth between us.

I felt Roger's eyes on me. Finally I raised my head and looked into his eyes. There was no trace of the cavalier coffee maker now, only the naked vulnerability of an honest man. Feeling my heart swell with gratitude, I smiled at him.

The room was filled with silence, not silence as in the absence of sound, but silence as in the stillness of beauty. It was almost dark, but there was enough light to see that everything was just the way I had left it. The chairs had been moved to one side, leaving a large open space on the floor, and a small vase of wildflowers stood surrounded by the three white votive candles in the centre of the altar. I lit the candles, their flickering light reflected off the gold, green and blue of the stained glass window. Roger, who had paused for a moment just inside the doorway, said, 'Oh, Maria, thank you for bringing me here. It is exquisite.'

I smiled, gesturing for him to join me. The two of us stood for a moment, watching the candlelight and shadows dance on the walls, then knelt side-by-side in front of the altar. I turned to look at Roger. His eyes were already closed, his hands laid palms down on his knees. Then, turning back to look at the cross hanging from the ceiling, I closed my eyes too. Inhaling deeply, then exhaling in a long, drawn-out breath, I felt my body relax and soften, realizing that, in this moment, I did not wish for anything else. Everything I loved, everything I had been or would someday be, was a part of the air I was now breathing. I closed my eyes and said a prayer silently in my heart.

'Thank you, thank you, thank you God, for this moment, for this place, for this life. May I remember, too, that everything that has happened until now, including Hannah's death, is a part of this moment I am now living, and had to happen in order to bring me here.'

I felt my body continue to settle into itself, my awareness becoming singularly focused on the slow, steady beat of my heart, the rise and fall of my breath. I lost track of time and of Roger's presence beside me. As my thoughts became like clouds across a summer sky, wafting through my mind, untouched, my sense of my self became more an energetic aliveness than a body, a separateness both independent from and connected to everything around me.

Gathering my attention, I knew without thinking that this feeling was the essence of who I was; it was the life energy that fuelled my body as it moved through the story of my life. My time on retreat wasn't about Claude, my kids or even Roger; it was about me returning to an awareness of myself, learning to trust my instincts as a woman, knowing that the most authentic expression of myself in my life could only be drawn from the source of this silence in me.

Silence

The house was quiet and smelled like ice ripening. I wrote in my journal and watched Hannah breathe. Baby Margaret was asleep on the bed next to Hannah. Her birth, exactly three weeks earlier, had seemed a bittersweet impossibility as it unfolded before our eyes. Hannah was thrilled, and insisted on coming to the hospital. 'It's what big sisters do,' she said. Although we didn't know it then, it turned out to be the last day Hannah left the house. The next day, she was in so much pain that, with the assistance of a hospice nurse, we had started her on morphine.

The circle of life had never been so evident to me. Even now, seeing Hannah's wasted body beside the plump, pinkness of the little sister she had so desperately wanted, my heart felt as if it might split in two. These days, while Margaret mostly nursed and slept, Hannah lay with her eyes closed in the middle of Claude's and my bed, dozing, barely speaking. Now, exhausted from too many sleepless nights, I closed my eyes and rocked, resting my head against the back of the chair.

Suddenly, Hannah moaned. My eyes flew open. Hannah was reaching for me. I jumped up, checking the morphine pump and IV line to make sure nothing had malfunctioned.

'Does it hurt, baby?' I asked, stroking the top of her head. 'Should I push the button and give you more morphine?'

Hannah nodded, still moaning and reaching for me. Starting to feel scared, I pushed the button. Although her condition had seemed stable when Dr Kamalaker stopped by the day before, something had drastically changed. I decided to pick her up, not knowing what else to do. I lifted her off the bed and sat on the edge of the mattress, resting her body on my lap. Placing a soft pillow between her head and my arm, I covered the rest of her with her pink blanket. Hannah stopped moaning. Although her breath sounded strange, rapid and shallow, her eyes were open, looking at me. I reached for the phone and called Claude at work.

'I think you should come home right away,' I said. Then I made two more calls: one to the hospice nurse and one to my friend Kate, asking her to come and help with Margaret, and asking her to arrange for our friend Lili to bring Will, who was at Lili's house, playing with her son Philippe.

Minutes later, I heard Kate's footsteps running up the stairs. When she opened the door and saw Hannah on my lap, she began to cry.

'Is this it?' she whispered.

'I don't know,' I said. Kate picked up Margaret.

'We'll wait downstairs,' she said. Just then, the door opened and Pat, the hospice nurse came in. Our eyes met, but neither of us said anything. She kneeled on the floor in front of me and gently examined Hannah who was now thrashing intermittently. When she looked up, she had tears in her eyes, and I knew. Paging Hannah's doctor, Pat quietly explained what was happening, listened for a moment, nodding, and then hung up. There was another tentative knock on the door. Will stepped into the room. He looked at Hannah on my lap, and then at me.

'Is it time, Mom?' he asked.

'Yes, Will,' I said.

Will bent down, stroked Hannah's hair, and kissed the top of her head.

'I love you, Hannah,' he said. Her eyes rolled toward him. The two of them looked at each other for a moment and then Will looked at me.

'Mom, I want to wait downstairs, but as soon as Hannah dies, come and get me, okay?'

I nodded. He kissed Hannah once more.

'Remember, Hannah, I love you,' he said, then turned and left the room.

Ten minutes later, Claude's car pulled into the driveway. The door slammed. I heard his footsteps thudding on the stairs. He threw open the door.

'What's happening?' he asked Pat, who was sitting on the floor with the morphine pump.

'Hannah's dying,' I said, more calmly than I could believe. 'She's been waiting for you. You have to tell her it's okay to go.'

Claude fell to his knees and let out a low moan. His body shook with sobs. He lifted his head, leaned over and kissed her. Up until this moment, while he had agreed that I should speak with Will and Hannah about the fact that Hannah was likely to die, he had been unable to speak to Hannah or anyone else about the one thing he could not bear – saying goodbye.

'It's time for you to go, Missy,' he said now. 'Don't worry about us. We love you. We're going to be okay.'

Although Hannah's body continued to fight for 20 minutes longer, some part of her already felt free, as if the life force inside and outside Hannah's body was who she was; her body seemed a separate thing. Then, one moment she was alive and breathing, the next, she wasn't. I couldn't believe how unexpected it felt. I looked into her eyes. Nothing but blue. The room had filled with an almost palpable stillness that enveloped us in its thick, white peace.

Frozen in Time

Claude, Will, and I were standing on the spot that would be Hannah's grave, gazing at the pond. We watched while one duck followed another across the surface of the water, and a slender white egret nosed its beak into the reeds along the far shore. I was holding baby Margaret, who was asleep in my arms, while Wanda, the cemetery manager, waited a discreet distance away.

The three of us, Claude, Will and I were making an almost impossible decision; we were deciding if this was the right place for Hannah's body to be buried. And if it were, this would be where Claude and I would be buried too. It was unconceivable to either of us that Hannah's body should spend eternity on its own.

'I think this is where Hannah should be buried,' Will said quietly, breaking the silence. 'She would like the pond, and my kids will be able to throw stones and stuff when I bring them here to see Hannah.' I bent down to give Will a hug, burying my face in his sweet-smelling hair, not wanting him to see any more tears.

'What do you think,' Claude asked me. Looking at him, I wondered if the despair and resignation was as obvious in my eyes. I turned and looked again at the slope of land as it emerged from the stand of pines and rolled downhill towards the plateau where we stood and then on to the edge of the pond.

I appreciated the way that this place didn't feel like a cemetery. Because the headstones and grave markers were laid flat on the ground, it looked more like a place for a picnic than a home for the dead. It was also true that everything about this spot spoke to me of another time and place, and I couldn't shake the feeling that I had been here before. While it was true that Claude and I had decided to bury Hannah in Ann Arbor, because it was where Will and Hannah had been born, where Claude and I had lived while he was in graduate school, and where we had owned our first home, I couldn't remember ever having visited a cemetery in the time we had lived here. I suspected that the feeling of familiarity was simply my way of trying to make it okay that we were planning to bury and leave Hannah's body in this spot, and then drive away.

'I think Will is right. Hannah would like it here,' I said. Claude nodded his head in agreement, and gave a thumbs-up sign to Wanda. I smiled gratefully at him. I knew he had really preferred the gravesite under the pines at the top of the hill, but we had agreed to let Will cast the final vote. There were so few things Will had been able to have a say in or control.

'Let's walk back through the pines before we return to the car,' I said. Will let out a whoop and raced ahead up the hill. Smiling with relief at having made such an enormous decision, Claude and I joined hands and began the climb. As we crested the hill and stepped into the shade of the trees, I suddenly remembered that Claude and I had been here before, and I knew why I hadn't fully realized it until now.

Something about the bend of the pines, the slope of the hill and the path through the trees touched a memory in me. On a grey winter afternoon, more than 10 years before, Claude had taken a break from his studies and invited me to go ice-skating with him on a pond he had noticed on his way home from class. Holding Claude's hand now, with Margaret in my other arm and Will running up ahead, I could still remember the feeling of my skates slung over my shoulder, the icy breath in my nostrils, and the chunks of snow dropping onto the path in front of us as we made our way home through the trees.

I knew, then, that this was where Hannah's body should be – in a place that could hold not only Will's hopes for the future, but also memories of a life Claude and I had known long ago.

Blanket of Grief

I woke in the middle of the night. Opening my eyes, there was no light in the room and no moon in the sky. I lay quietly for a moment, and then realized what had woken me. Claude, lying next to me in the bed, was quietly sobbing into his pillow. I rolled towards him until my body was stretched alongside his. Lifting my arm from beneath the blankets and laying it across his chest, I felt his whole body begin shaking, as he knew I was awake and no longer had to subdue his tears.

There are no words for the dark spaces between breaths where Claude and I went in the first months and years after Hannah's death. Grief was a blanket that enveloped and suffocated us. Watching the casket bearing Hannah's body being lowered into the ground, I had felt everything I knew or trusted about my self and my life fall away. The single-minded focus on Hannah and our family that I had maintained in the last year of Hannah's life vanished. In its place I was left with a sense that my mind had been completely disconnected from my body. Caring for Margaret and Will was the best and only thing I seemed to be able to do. And although Claude had returned to work a week and a half after Hannah died, he too seemed to be going through the motions of a meaningless life.

'I think it was my fault she died,' Claude whispered now, as if the words were too terrible to say aloud. 'I should have been a better person, closer to God. I prayed everyday, but I started too late. It wasn't enough.'

I began to cry too, as my own guilt and grief broke open in me. Although I had barely wanted to name the truth in my heart, since the moment we heard that Hannah's tumour was in her left kidney, I had felt that Hannah had sacrificed herself to the anger in me that could not be assuaged. How else could God justify taking such a pure and joyful life? Holding Claude's broken body in my arms, I felt breathless in the face of life's cruelty. I ached for what Claude, Will and I now knew about the hopelessness and helplessness of being human and alive. And I ached for everything we would never know: why Hannah died and other children didn't, Hannah as a ballerina, Hannah aged 12.

'I've been thinking all this time it was my fault,' I said, taking deep breaths between sobs in order to get the words out. 'I can't forget the image of her on the steps in the family room that day. But I also can't believe that the God I love would punish us by punishing her. Maybe, if there is a reason, it's something we simply will never be able to understand.'

'Well, I can't accept that there is no reason,' Claude said. 'But I also know that Hannah would not want us to be angry because she died. I think the only thing we can do is try to be better people because we love Hannah, and because she was so good.'

I understood how Claude felt. I had been praying ever since Hannah's death that each of us, having been stripped of everything that mattered except our children and each other, might somehow find a way to care about life again, to learn from our mistakes and shortcomings and become better partners, better parents. But I was afraid, too, that our guilt and anger in response to Hannah's death might have hardened our hearts and further widened the gap between us. Closing my eyes, feeling Claude's body next to mine, now softened and quiet, I felt comforted by his presence but also broken open to a deeper loneliness. I knew now that there was no assuaging another person's guilt or grief. And although Claude and I could not be more together in our shared suffering and missing Hannah, we also could not be more alone.

Friday

I WATCHED AS THE SPIDER DANGLED PRECARIOUSLY ON HER almost invisible thread, then swung wide, catching the outside edge of her web. I challenged myself to notice every detail of her movement, knowing there was beauty in each one. Finally, my eyes tired, I leaned back in the rocking chair in the shade of the cabin's porch roof and took a bite of my apple, grateful that I had decided to spend another day in the woods.

I was completely enjoying being on my own, and savouring the way my thoughts could chase themselves from one point to the next, without any chance of being interrupted. I hadn't fully realized, until now, the way that, even as a young girl, my attention was always diverted from what I thought was interesting or important. I had come to believe that it was my responsibility to respond with interest, even if it was feigned, to whatever my mother, father, husband or children were interested in; my own thoughts took a back seat to everyone else's. What had surprised me most, though, in the silence and solitude of these past few days, was that the movement of my thoughts was often even more interesting than the specifics of the thoughts themselves.

And yet, as much as I loved being on my own, I also missed my kids. I had spoken to them and my sister several times in the past days. They had been happy to hear my voice, but were having too much fun to speak with me for long. Laura had assured me the time was passing quickly for them, and everything was going well.

Even so, I still found myself wondering about them, Claude and even Roger. It seemed that although I was appreciating having this stretch of time to myself, there was a large part of me that loved relationship and being part of a community. I could see now that there wasn't just one thing I needed. Different movements, like tides, were continually shifting back and forth in me, running first towards wanting to be with another, and then turning back towards a desire for solitude.

The way that Roger and I had met and become friends seemed to reinforce that point. But what now seemed peculiar, or even perhaps magical, was how each of us had ended up here during the same week. My sister, Laura, had offered at Christmas to give me the gift of the retreat I had been talking about for years. It was she and her manager at the bank who had determined that these 10 days in July were the best time for Laura to take off work to watch my kids. I had made reservations to stay at this particular centre after seeing a write-up about it in a library book.

Roger, on the other hand, had originally planned to stay for a month at another retreat, just over the road. A week before he was scheduled to leave, they had called him to say they had overbooked the first 10 days of his stay. They had made reservations for him at another retreat centre for those days. That's how we ended up both staying here at the same time.

Now, rocking on the porch of the cabin, I could not ignore the synchronicity that our visits had overlapped in the same week; nor could I stop my mind from wondering what it might mean.

I stepped out of the shower and reached for a towel as drops of water slid down my back and legs onto the cool tile floor. The afternoon's humidity had chased me from the porch, and left me feeling as if only the coldest shower would clear my mind. Wiping my body dry, I wrapped the towel around my hair, brushed my teeth and began smoothing lavender-scented lotion over my arms and legs. As my hands slid along my limbs, out of the corner of my eye I saw my reflection in the mirror. Almost shyly, I turned and stood up straight. Mesmerized, I could not remember the last time I had really looked at my body.

My eyes travelled over my form, across my strong shoulders, past my small, soft breasts, touch-sensitive nipples, firm, flat stomach and child-bearing hips. I allowed my glance to linger on my triangle patch of pubic hair before continuing down towards my long, strong legs and solid, man-sized feet. Extending my hands, I studied them too. Of all the parts of

my body, they were the most familiar: long, strong and capable, they were not only the hands of a lover, mother, healer
and woman, they were also the hands of a poet, gardener,
explorer, writer and painter – aspects of myself that I had yet
to express or explore.

Staring at myself in the mirror, I marvelled that this body
was capable of closing around my lover as he entered me, as
well as opening wide to deliver four babies into the world. I
thought of how, in the busyness of my days, I often willed my
body not to need anything. Distracted by my compulsion to
take care of everyone and everything else, I often forgot to
eat, refused to sit down and willed myself not to go to the
bathroom for hours. Seeing my body now, as a vulnerable,
beautiful receptacle for the energy and movement of my life,
I vowed I would take better care of myself, listen more attentively to what my body needed. 'Thank you,' I whispered,
wanting to cry, except that I was smiling too widely to
make tears.

The setting sun was catching the fields on fire as I made my
way back to the centre's barn. Swinging my pack in one
hand, I walked slowly, the way I imagined Native Americans
did, so as not to frighten the small animals, insects and birds
that darted across the path.

After a day sitting quietly on the front porch of the cabin,
all my senses were heightened. The resonance of belonging I
had felt in the chapel the night before had expanded to

include every living thing: the light, the sky, the earth and the trees. I loved the way this retreat was not only helping to ignite important memories in me, but as I had in the past day begun again writing notes for the book about Hannah's life, it was also clear that it was inspiring me to move more wholly and fully in the direction of my unlived dreams.

Rounding the corner of the barn, I had nearly reached the door, when I heard a shout. Turning, I saw Roger running towards me, grinning and waving like a 12-year-old kid. He must have spotted me from the window in his room. I had to laugh. More than once in the past couple of days, I had passed this way in the afternoon, secretly hoping he would see me and come down. Now, when I had no such thought in my mind, it had happened.

'Hello, Maria!' he said, breathlessly, giving me a quick hug. 'I missed you at dinner this evening.' He paused to catch his breath. 'I was wondering, if you're not too tired and it's not too late, if you might like to amble.'

I smiled, appreciating how handsome he looked in his white linen shirt, his expectant blue eyes twinkling at me.

'Sure, I'd love to,' I said.

'Oh good! Here, let me take that for you,' Roger replied, reaching for my backpack. He opened the door to the barn and disappeared inside. A few moments later, he returned.

'I put it on the floor in your room,' he said.

'Thank you,' I said, taking his hand. The two of us looked at each other and smiled. Suddenly, it felt the simplest, most natural thing for my hand to be held in his. I couldn't help wondering if he was thinking the same thing.

The light of the moon served to guide us as we picked our way carefully along the path. For the next half hour, we walked in silence. I felt particularly attuned to Roger's presence. There was a thrumming awareness, so palpable between us, that I began to feel its energy *was* Roger and I.

Too soon, it seemed, we had completed the path's circle and returned to the barn. Before opening the door, Roger stopped and turned. Although I could only see the outline of his form in the moonlight, I could feel his eyes travelling over me. My body began to shake in anticipation, like a teenager on a first date. I was sure he could feel the pounding of my heart in my chest as he moved close enough for us to inhale and exhale the same breath. Staring into my eyes, he slowly began to run his hands along the sides of my face, then over my shoulders and arms, and, finally, encircling my waist.

'Do you have any idea how beautiful you are?' he whispered. I felt my eyes fill with tears as I inhaled the muskiness of his scent.

Reaching my arms around his neck, I allowed him to pull me close. My lips could feel the warmth of his, but still they didn't touch.

'Thank you for this time we've had together,' he said quietly. 'I think it's best, though, that we don't ask for it to be more than this.'

My mind suspected he was probably right, but as I lay in the dark of my room more than an hour later, savouring the memory of his heart beating against my chest, my body was still trembling.

Dancing with Love

We were swaying back and forth to the music, having spontaneously come together as each of us was getting dressed and ready for the day. My arms were wrapped around Claude's neck, and his were pulling me close at the small of my back. I shut my eyes and lay my cheek on his shoulder.

More than two and a half years after Hannah's death, it seemed a miracle, not only that Claude and I had managed to regain our footing and re-emerge into the world and each other, but we had also created another new life between us. A little over a year after Hannah's death, our daughter Madelaine was born. Deciding to have another child had been a huge decision for Claude and I to make. But both of us felt strongly that without another baby, our family was incomplete. It also felt as if our marriage and family had been opened to new sense of hope and possibility, having made such an abrupt, unexpected turn.

Holding Madelaine for the first time, feeling the grasp of her tiny hand around my finger, I had looked into Claude's teary eyes and known that she was the last baby we needed to have. I felt complete as a mother and happier than I had even been. In moments like that, and the one Claude and I were dancing in now, I realized that having negotiated such a dark path together, Claude and I had discovered a new respect for what we could accomplish as a team, and forged a bond stronger than all the anger and immaturity we had experienced. Claude, I knew, was the only person in the world who would ever appreciate how much I had lost and changed since Hannah's death. And after the loneliness and heartache I had experienced, the love we knew with each other and for Hannah, Will, Margaret and

Madelaine meant more to me now than it ever had before.

I heard Will's footsteps pounding up the steps to our room, and then pause in the doorway. Opening my eyes, I turned my head to smile at him. He grinned at me, his eyes alive and shining as he watched Claude and me dance.

'Hey, Buddy,' Claude said, 'Do you want to join us?' Will nodded his head and then stepped shyly into our embrace, wrapping his arms around both our legs. As we held on to each other, the song ended and another began. The three of us continued to dance.

'This feels good,' Will said finally, giving our legs a squeeze. Claude and I laughed and kissed each other lightly. Then, readjusting his grip on my body, Claude whispered in my ear, 'I wonder if its time for us to start shopping for your new wedding ring.'

I opened my eyes and looked into his. Smiling, I said teasingly, 'Yes, and you can give it to me when we renew our vows.'

Claude laughed and poked me in the ribs. This had become our shared joke, that I had begun to have an image of myself in a grown-up wedding with my kids as attendants, rather than the one Claude and I had had, with homemade bridesmaid's dresses in dusty rose satin, that I'd planned in my head when I was 16 years old. Claude wasn't sure he was ready for another ceremony, but the one thing we did seem to agree on was that neither of us had ever been crazy about the setting of the thin, white gold engagement ring Claude had given me when he proposed. He explained, when he first slipped it on my finger, that the small but beautiful diamond was what he had carefully chosen – the setting, he wanted me to choose. But, ever the romantic, I had insisted I wanted to wear the exact ring Claude had given me, even though I had always imagined my wedding ring as a thick, yellow gold band.

Now, though, twirling together in the middle of our bedroom with Will's arms wrapped around our legs, I realized that renewing our vows or getting a new ring really wasn't that important to me. What mattered was this life and family Claude and I were still creating together, and while it was far from perfect, we continued to share a commitment to making it work.

Ring of Fire

I ran the dust rag along the edge of Claude's dresser and underneath the homemade picture frame and photo of Will he had received as his first Father's Day gift when Will was one year-old. There was one item on Claude's dresser, though, that I hesitated to touch. If I wasn't mistaken, Claude's white gold wedding band had been sitting in the exact same spot when I dusted a week before. Lifting the ring carefully from the dresser, its tell-tale imprint on the dusty surface told me what I needed to know. I felt sick to my stomach. There was no room for this in the story I had dreamed of my life.

Balancing the ring on the tip of my index finger, I listened to the sounds of Claude getting ready for work in the bathroom and the faint strains of cartoon music wafting up the stairs from the television room. One part of me wasn't surprised by this turn of events. Not long ago, Claude had turned 40. Soon afterwards, he purchased a weight-lifting machine, and besides lifting weights every day, he also started reading books from a list of 100 classics, emphatically insisting that I should be reading them too.

Inhaling a shaky breath, I was still trying to decide what to say, when the bathroom door opened. Claude stopped three steps in when he saw the look in my eyes and his wedding ring dangling from the finger of my right hand. His face was expressionless as he stared at me.

'You haven't been wearing it, have you?' I asked quietly. He didn't respond, not even a nod. The two of us continued to stare at each other: me confused and wondering, him defiant. Claude turned, walked to his dresser and took a pair of socks from his drawer.

'Why?' I asked, 'Why aren't you wearing your wedding ring?'

Claude refused to look at me. I watched as he sat on the edge of the bed and put on his socks, and then stood up, pulling on his trousers. Finally he spoke.

'It's not that I want a divorce,' he said, his voice measured and terse, 'But in general I am still very dissatisfied with the way you conduct yourself as a wife. I will not put my wedding ring on again until you are the kind of woman I want to be married to.'

I felt as if I had been slapped in the face. I could still see the list of needs Claude had handed me a few weeks before. Most of his requests, wanting the bathroom to himself in the morning, his dress shirts washed and ironed in the same day, and 15–20 minutes on his own when he first got home from work, I felt willing to respect and accept. But his need to have sex with me every day as a way to address the lack of love and connection he was feeling in relation to me was something I had told him I felt uneasy about. It was as if he were asking me to pour myself into a hole he had dug himself, setting me up to fail by asking me to heal a wound that could never heal.

Now, staring at Claude, I felt my body contract as I attempted to get a hold of the anger rising in me. I wanted to lunge at him – or crumple to the floor and cry. But I could see in Claude's eyes that he was impervious to any response I might make. So, without saying anything, I returned the ring to the top of his dresser and walked out of the room. I couldn't help wondering, as I made my way downstairs, how we could go on for so long, feeling as if things were good and right between us, and then, in a blink of an eye, realize that what we shared was simply an idea. And no matter how frightening it was, I also knew that regardless of what dreams I had for my life or marriage, Claude's life was his to live. I had no control over what he might or might not choose to do.

Foreign Language

I turned the envelope over in my hands, looking for clues. It had arrived in our mailbox, wedged between an electric bill and a credit card offer from our bank. It was handwritten in a loopy, feminine scrawl on lightweight airmail paper, and addressed to CLAUDE ALAN MARTELL. I didn't have to guess where it was from. Claude had recently returned not long ago from a business trip to Germany and I was almost certain I knew something about the person who had sent it. Only a woman who had known intimacy with a man would have cared to know his middle name.

Standing in the front hall, I carefully considered whether to open the envelope and read the letter inside. I held the letter up to the light, but was unable to distinguish any of the words. Although part of me didn't want to wait for Claude to come home and risk him not telling me the truth about the envelope's contents, I also knew that my integrity meant even more to me now I was holding evidence that Claude might have compromised his.

Something about Claude had felt foreign to me ever since his return. While I had been excited to see him, having experienced an increased sense of love and appreciation for him during the time he'd been away, Claude had seemed unusually distracted and vulnerable. When I had asked him, our first night together, about his time in Germany, he had been sketchy and elusive. He did admit that being away from me, our home and family had given him a new perspective on his life, but he had also assured me that the shift he was feeling wasn't about anything that had happened in Germany.

Hearing his words, my heart had opened to him even more. I had held him in my arms for a long time, and then, tenderly, gently, we had made love. The next day, after work, Claude had pulled a box of cassette tapes out of his briefcase. It was an introductory course on how to speak German. 'I want to learn how to speak another language,' was his only explanation. I hoped it might mean we were one step closer to taking the vacation to Europe we had sometimes talked about.

Now, going on vacation with Claude, no matter where it was, was the last thing I wanted to do. More than ever I needed to get away, to have some time and space on my own. Fortunately, only two months before, my sister Laura had offered to watch my kids for 10 days in July so I could go on a retreat. The timing couldn't have been more perfect. Curling up into a tiny ball on our bed, tears streaming down my cheeks, I willed myself to hold on until then.

Saturday

⸻

THE MORNING SUN WAS STREAMING THROUGH THE CURTAINED windows when I woke. I stretched the length of my body and groaned contentedly, grateful to have slept in. Leaning back against a pile of pillows, I replayed my memories of the night before, of Roger's hands on my body, still feeling a visceral connection with him. Suddenly, my reverie was interrupted by a knock on the door.

'Just a minute,' I called out, leaping out of bed and throwing on my robe.

Grinning with anticipation, I pulled the door open. Roger was standing there, wearing a t-shirt, shorts and running shoes, but when I saw the serious look on his face, I lost my smile.

'Is everything okay?' I asked, holding the door open wider. 'Would you like to come in?'

Roger nodded his head, and stepped into the room. I closed the door and turned to him. His posture was stiff, arms hanging at his side, fists clenched as if he was steeling himself for what he was about to say. His eyes, looking into mine, were cloudy with seriousness. My heart suddenly felt like a stone in my chest.

'I hardly slept last night. I need your help,' he said, running his hands nervously from the top of his head down to his neck. He cleared his throat, and continued, 'Sometimes the greatest offering we can make to love is to say "no". So what I need, what I think both our lives need, is for you to help me say "no" to what is happening between us.'

The stone in my heart dropped with a thud into my gut. I searched his face for any sign of the joy we had shared the night before, but it was not there. He was silent, now looking more determined than sad, but I made no attempt to hide the hurt in my eyes. Although I felt chastised by him, disappointed, I also realized that part of me had been expecting this and probably even agreed.

I looked away, into the distance outside my window, and took a deep breath. Even though every cell in my body was screaming 'No', I turned back to him, tears in my eyes, and said in the lifeless, you–can't–hurt–me voice that I recognized from my other life, 'Yes. I'll help you with what you asked.'

I pried two rusty thumbtacks from the wall and, letting the screen door slam shut behind me, descended the porch steps and walked back to where the path leading to the cabin turned off from the main trail. There I found a suitable tree and tacked two white index cards to it. The first read, 'This Way' with an arrow pointing in the direction of the cabin, the second, 'Enter at your own risk', with a smiley face below. I wasn't sure if Roger had been to the cabin before, and since I knew in my heart he would come, I wanted to make it as easy as possible for him to find me.

Stepping back to admire my handiwork, I heard a rustle of leaves. I turned, expecting to see Roger, but instead a doe and her spotted fawn emerged into the late morning light from the shadow of the trees. For a long, silent moment, the three of us stared at each other, and then, with a flick of their white tails, the deer disappeared into the woods.

As I strolled back to the cabin, I felt grateful for the way its sanctuary and the skittering, chattering, busyness of the forest had helped me regain the composure I had lost two hours before. As soon as Roger had left my room, I had hurriedly packed a bag with some food, slipped a note under his door telling him I was going to the cabin, and ran through the woods. Blinded by tears and numb with disappointment, I hadn't felt the thorns as they ripped through the skin on my bare ankles. Only later, sitting on the front porch had I noticed the rivulets of dry blood.

For an hour, I laid face down on the bed in the cabin, screaming and sobbing into the pillows. I had felt as if the only part of my heart that had not broken after Hannah's death was now split in two. Roger's words had stung; I felt a silly, childish schoolgirl for the secret wishes I had harboured, and grateful that what the two of us had shared the previous night hadn't developed into more. Yet, once my tears had dried, I realized that I wanted Roger to change his mind.

Now, returning to the cabin, I ate my lunch of fruit and

cheese. I stared out the window, watching the path, and imagined that Roger must be missing me terribly and regretting what he had said. I felt certain that if his feelings were even half the intensity of mine, it wouldn't be long before he would make his way to me. After eating, I cleaned my dishes, filled one of the mugs with fresh flowers and placed it in the centre of the table. Looking around the room, I wondered where I should be when Roger arrived.

'Who am I fooling?' I said aloud. Like every one of my favourite movies, I knew how the story was supposed to unfold. Climbing on top of the bed, I was careful not to muss the covers as I lay down and closed my eyes, just like Sleeping Beauty, certain that our happily-ever-after was assured.

I awoke two hours later, disoriented for a moment by my surroundings. As soon as I realized where I was, I jumped off the bed. Glancing around the cabin, I saw that everything was exactly as I had left it. Opening the door, I stepped onto the porch. A large blue jay, startled by my sudden appearance, cried out from his perch on a nearby branch and, flapping his wings, flew up and away. Walking quickly along the path, I saw in the distance the white of the index cards still tacked to the trees, but no sign of Roger. For a brief moment, I allowed myself to imagine he had either made a late start or was now hopelessly lost in the woods. But the sinking feeling in my stomach was telling another, much different story: Roger had clearly made his decision – he was not going to come.

Making my way back to the cabin, I sat on the edge of the bed, feeling such a tumble of emotions that I couldn't even cry. Unlike the way in which I had succumbed to the hysterical, all-consuming impulse that had inspired me to race to the cabin that morning, I knew I now had to be absolutely certain of how I really felt and what really mattered before deciding what to do next. I willed myself to a quieter, more thoughtful task. With an unexpected sense of curiosity and calm, I began to turn my feelings over in my mind, fingering them and then setting them down, like stones on the beach.

At first glance, I felt hurt and rejected that Roger had not come, and was certain it was somehow my fault. I had never before in my life attempted to initiate something like this and I couldn't help thinking that my naiveté had contributed to events. Perhaps he had been put off by the evident hurt in my eyes that morning, or maybe the intensity of my feelings had scared him. I wished now that I had appeared less obvious, more independent, or braver. I felt silly and foolish for having opened myself so much to him, and now wondered if it had been a mistake.

And yet, even as this thought crossed my mind, I knew it wasn't true. I really *did not* regret being so honest and open with him. I felt proud of the way I had conducted myself, and knew that everything I had said and done had come from an inner sense of clarity and confidence. I had never before felt so comfortable in my life, so beautiful and sure in my body. No matter what did or did not happen with Roger, nothing could change that.

Standing up, I began to pace back and forth across the room, charged, unusually restless. It was as if I was watching a crack in my shell slowly widening, seeing new aspects of myself revealed. Most surprising was that I did not feel ashamed of my behaviour, of my wish to be with a man other than my husband. I had always prided myself on being a good, moral, upstanding person. I felt nothing like the kind of bold, uncaring, irresponsible woman who I imagined committed adultery. Adultery, I had always believed, was a sin against God, and yet, despite or perhaps because of what was happening, I felt closer than ever to Him.

Snippets of every lecture my father had given me about the evils of premarital sex, and previous unfounded accusations Claude has made, now whispered in my ear. All my life, those voices had demanded that I subdue any part of myself that might be expressed erotically. And because I had believed I had to be 'good' in order to be loved, I had obeyed.

I now realized that this morning had been no exception. I had come to the cabin not because I wanted to be there, but because I thought Roger had wanted me to. I had believed he simply needed time and space away from me to think things through, and my fantasy was that because I had been so obedient, he would 'reward' me by coming.

Sitting on the edge of the bed, I stared out the window at the empty path. Years of frustration and anger welled up, and I felt an overwhelming sense of powerlessness. It was as if I had been waiting on the edge of that bed forever, believing that someone else would have to do something or something else would have to happen before my 'real' life could begin. Like a barometer, I had allowed my actions to be dictated by the wants and needs of others, secretly hoping that if I were good enough and patient enough, something good would happen. I was always on the cusp of something bigger and better. The held breath of 'any moment now' was as familiar to me as the pause of my heart between beats.

Closing my eyes, I took a long, slow breath and felt my heart soften as I inched closer to its deepest secret. What if I had got it all wrong, if all these years I had completely missed the point of my life? What if it didn't have anything to do with waiting, with trying to be good? My eyes flew open. There was such a sense of clarity and purity in this realization that I knew that it was true. This room, this body and these feelings right here, right now, *were* my life. Whether good or bad, perfect or imperfect, what mattered wasn't about what happened outside myself or whether others approved; what mattered was how fully and unapologetically I was able to be who I was.

Staring into nothing, I felt my heart beating in my chest, my breath drawing in and out of my lungs, and every inch of my body tingling with sensation. I had lived so much of my life feeling under the thumb of someone else – first my parents and then Claude – that it had taken me until now to realize that regardless of what other people thought I should or shouldn't do, it was *I* who got to choose! I knew then that the most beautiful and vibrant part of myself was this creative, sexual, life-affirming energy. I could feel it calling me into a new kind of courage in my life, and even if others, including Roger, felt threatened or overwhelmed by it, I needed to trust it more and more.

Finally knowing what I needed to do, I packed the remains of my lunch in my bag, turned off the light and closed the door. I set off on the path towards the retreat centre, knowing that what my life was wanting had nothing to do with whether or not Roger and I would ever make love. Without needing or even caring to know what might happen as a result, I simply knew that I could no longer say 'no' to what was happening. Roger was free to make his own decision, but I had to trust this new sense of courage and determination I was feeling and stop allowing my fear to keep me from living.

I tapped lightly on his door and heard him call for me to come in. He was seated in front of his computer, in the soft light of the afternoon sun. As he turned to look at me, he was not smiling. Neither was I, but my body felt strong and tall, my feet were firmly planted, and I knew I could deeply trust what I was about to do.

'I thought you went to the cabin,' Roger said, standing and moving towards me, his lips pressed tightly together. From the tone of his voice, I could tell he was exasperated.

'I did,' I said. I took a deep breath, feeling carefully for the right words. 'I came back because the more I thought about it, the more I realized that I was there not because I wanted to be, but because I thought *you* wanted me to be.'

Roger cocked his head, studying my face. I took another deep breath and forged ahead.

'I'm sorry I interrupted you. I know you're busy. I just had to tell you one thing.' Roger's face was a blank canvas. I realized he had no idea what I was going to say.

'This morning you asked me to help you say "no" to what is happening.' I stopped as my voice faltered and tears began to well up in my eyes. I swallowed and cleared my throat, willing myself not to cry.

'I cannot help you with what you asked,' I said.

For a long moment, neither of us moved, my words resonating in the space between us. Finally Roger spoke.

'What do you mean,' he asked; the tone of his voice, gentle, soft and measured, suggested he already knew. Looking into his eyes, I felt the ground under my feet and the clarity in my heart.

'I am not afraid,' I said. 'I deeply trust what is happening right now, in me and in my life. I have room for you to do whatever is best for you, for you to say "no" if you need to. But I have to say "yes" – "yes" to my life, "yes" to whatever is happening between us.'

As the last word dropped from my lips, tears began to slide down my cheeks. I knew that, other than the moment of my children's births and Hannah's death, I had never been so close to God. I had just spoken the deepest truth in me, and in the face of its fierce gaze, everything less true in my life fell away.

Stepping forward, Roger opened his arms and wrapped them around me. As my body softened into his embrace, the story of my afternoon at the cabin poured out of me. I told him everything, the history of my regrets, my disappointments at not having had more courage, the way I knew I could no longer say 'no' to the most beautiful and true parts of me, that I could no longer worry about doing the 'right thing'.

While I spoke, Roger listened, nodding his head thoughtfully. At one point, he fetched a washcloth from the bathroom and, as the words continued to tumble out of me, used it to dry my tears and clean the dripping mascara off my cheeks. I was so immersed in telling my story, I hardly noticed Roger brushing his teeth, splashing cologne on his neck, and then, his hand pressed firmly against the small of my back, gently guiding me ahead of him up the stairs.

Not until we were sitting side-by-side on the edge of his bed, did I return to my body and register where I was. I fell silent then and glancing around his room, noticed his clothes thrown over the backs of chairs, a few candles and a stick of incense burning, the rumpled sheets on his unmade bed. I turned to look at Roger. The light in his eyes was as soft as moonlight as he lay back, pulling me towards him. For a long time, the two of us lay there, breathing as one breath, inhaling the peace that had descended between us.

Finally, I rolled my body over, towards him, our faces almost touching. I studied the lines in the corners of his eyes and traced with my finger the bow of his lips.

'You see,' I whispered, 'This is all I needed. This, right here, is enough.'

He smiled, then first softly, then more firmly touched his lips to mine. Returning his kisses, my body began to press against his. Pausing, Roger pulled his face away, his eyes dancing.

'I thought you said that holding each other was enough,' he said, playfully.

'It was,' I said, lightly kissing the top of his nose. 'But this is much better.'

Hollow Truth

The lamp on Will's bedside table cast its soft light across the pages of Farmer Boy *by Laura Ingalls Wilder, the book Will and I had been reading together. Beside me on the bed, Will's eyes were slowly closing. I loved the feeling of his warm, soft form next to mine. Although he was now 10 years old, there remained a sweetness and innocence in him that I treasured, as well as a maturity that threatened to break my heart.*

Watching him play basketball with his friends, listening to him tell me about a video game's complicated moves, or overhearing him sharing a story about Hannah with his sisters, I felt a sense of pride and respect for the young man he was becoming. Wrapping my arms around him, I held him close as he lay quietly with his head nestled into the space between my shoulder and chin.

'I love you, Mom,' he said.

'I love you too, Muffin,' I said, kissing him twice on each cheek. 'I think it's time to say goodnight.' Will smiled at me sleepily and held his floppy, blue bunny up to my face.

'Don't forget, Mom, Bunny needs a kiss too.' I smiled and dropped a kiss on the tip of the bunny's nose. Will grinned, and readjusted the bunny beside him under the blankets, then rolled over onto his side.

'Mom,' he asked in a quiet voice, as I reached for the light's switch 'Are you and Dad going to get a divorce?'

My arm froze in mid-air. Lately, although Claude and I had resumed marriage counselling, there was no hiding from our kids the difficulties we were having. Although Claude had insisted that he and the German woman who sent him the letter had dated and kissed but not had sex, I found the idea that Claude had even considered being with someone else difficult to accept. Ironically, I had spent years reassuring him that I would never commit adultery, because he had so frequently insisted I was going to leave him for another man.

The tension between us was stretched further because Claude's idea of what made a good wife seemed less and less what I wanted to be. Despite the therapist's help, the arguments between us were as loud and ugly as ever, the intensity and consistency of our anger towards each other matching the frustration we both seemed to feel.

Now, looking into Will's eyes, I knew his question was understandable, even inevitable, but because of the quiet of the house and the simplicity of the moment, it had caught me off guard. Taking a deep breath, I prayed for the right words and tried to imagine how uncertain and confused he must feel. It was not that long ago he had wrapped his arms around our legs as the three of us danced together. He was probably wondering why the pendulum between his parents seemed to swing so far from one side to the other. But as I struggled to find the words to reassure him, I felt constricted by my own uncertainty. How could I ever explain it to Will when I could not even understand it myself?

The mystery of why we were together had been answered at the moment of Hannah's death and at each of our four children's births. If it wasn't for our children, I was certain that we would not be together, but because of them, we wanted to understand why our being together could feel both right and wrong, at the same time.

Reaching for Will, I gathered him into my arms again and gave him another, bigger hug.

'I'm sorry for how painful and confusing all of this must feel to you, Will,' I said, trying not to cry. 'Even I don't understand why Dad and I are having so much trouble. But the one thing I know is that, even though we don't do it very well, we love each other. And more than anything else, we definitely love each of you kids. I can promise you that Dad and I are doing everything we can to work things out. Neither of us wants to get a divorce.'

I felt Will's body relax in my arms, as I continued to hold him.

'Thanks, Mom. That's what I needed to hear,' Will said, wiping his eyes and laying back down. Kissing him once more and then turning off the light, I was pleased that Will seemed relieved by my answer, but my words still echoed hollowly in my head.

Reality Interrupted

The other mothers and I could barely hear each other speak over the noise our children were making. Sitting next to Elizabeth, I sighed, exasperated that it was taking me so long to get to the end of the story I was telling. Constantly interrupted by one child or another, we had started and stopped our conversation in the middle of a sentence too many times to count.

My life, it seemed, had become a stream of interruptions. I could barely complete a thought. Whether it was the phone ringing, the clothes dryer buzzing or some question only I could answer, my attention was constantly being redirected from I was doing to what someone else wanted me to do. This morning, it had taken me two and a half hours to get Will off to school and Margaret and Madelaine dressed and fed. Five minutes before we were supposed to leave for playgroup, the girls were ready, but I hadn't yet brushed my teeth or changed out of my pyjamas. And I was not proud of the way I had begun to express my frustration. More than once in the past month, I had stood in front of Claude or one of my kids, screaming, 'Leave me alone' at the top of my voice.

Many of the bereaved moms I knew had spent weeks after their child's death, refusing to get out of bed or hiding in the bottom of a dark closet. My life hadn't afforded me that possibility, and I felt that meant my children had suffered more than they needed to due to my own shortcomings and lack of energy. I was anxious to go on my retreat, in order to rest and figure out what needed to happen next. I also longed for simple comforts – to be able to sleep in, not have to worry about making a meal or to have to pick up after anyone else. Life without Hannah would only be bearable if I could integrate what she had taught me about being honest, about what mattered, so my children might have the mother they needed and deserved.

Interrupting my reverie, Elizabeth caught my eye.

'If you could be granted one wish right now, what would it be?' she asked. I closed my eyes briefly, and immediately saw myself lying in the blazing sun on a deserted white sand beach, a gentle breeze blowing in off a sapphire blue sea.

'A week of solitude on a remote Caribbean island,' I said.

Elizabeth laughed out loud. 'Oh, Maria, you are so funny,' she giggled.

'Why? What would you wish for?' I asked, sensing I had once again missed part of the conversation.

'Oh, that's easy,' Elizabeth wasn't laughing now. 'I'd wish for a lifetime of happiness for each of my kids.'

I smiled through my teeth, but said, 'Fuck, fuck, fuck' under my breath. I was sick and tired of getting questions like that wrong.

A New Leaf

The air was cool, but the dark soil, warmed by the sun, felt good in my hands. I had not realized until now that a soil's richness can be determined not only by its colour, but also by its heft and weight, the pungency of its scent and the ease with which it parts to let a plants roots in. For years, the idea of planting a garden had been turning over in my mind. Like painting, though, I had imagined that it required lots of understanding and skill, and was therefore something I would only be able to do when I had more time. But lately, feeling restless and disconnected from life, I had spent hours looking out the window, watching crocus push their heads above ground and the trees unfurling their new leaves. I had decided I needed something new to occupy my thoughts, and planting a garden seemed the right thing.

Now, poking little pockets into the earth with my fingers, and dropping in pearls of seeds, I felt grateful to be doing something so hands-on and productive. I could already imagine myself this summer, filling vases with my own fresh flowers, watching my kids pull new carrots from the earth and snap ripe tomatoes from their stems. One of my favourite aspects of this garden had nothing to do with its flowers, herbs, and vegetables, though. A secret path of flat stones wove in and out through the plantings, leading to a tiny stone angel and birdbath in the middle, a simple memorial to Hannah.

Standing up, bending the tension out of my back, I smiled at Margaret and Madelaine who, with their sand shovels, had dug a hole big enough for a small tree in one corner of the garden, and were now filling it with packets of leftover seeds and handfuls of grass and twigs. The two of them, now two and three years old respectively, were rarely separated; it seemed they had been best friends since birth. Only sixteen months apart, many people automatically assumed they were twins, not necessarily because they looked alike, but because their delight in being together was obvious, and the connection between them so unique.

'Hey, you two,' I called out from my side of the garden, 'How's it going over there?'

'Good, Mommy,' Margaret said, as Madelaine, at the sound of my voice, stood up and began waving her shovel in my direction. 'Come see. Me and Maddy are making some garden soup.'

Smiling, I made my way toward them. Both girls were now squatting beside the edge of the huge hole they had dug. 'Here Maddy,' Margaret said, handing Madelaine an enormous stick, 'you're the littlest so you can stir first.'

It was one of those moments where the whole scene unfolds in the mind, seconds before it actually happens. Before I could stop her, Madelaine reached both hands out towards Margaret and took the stick from her. Because Madelaine was already squatting and leaning too close to the edge of the hole, the weight of the stick tipped the balance. Margaret and I watched helplessly as Madelaine tumbled into the bed of grass, leaves, and twigs at the bottom of the hole.

'Don't worry, Maddy, I'll save you,' Margaret shouted, scrambling to a standing position and jumping feet first, as if off a diving board, into the pit with Madelaine.

'Oh, my goodness,' I said, finally reaching them and leaning over to lift them out. 'Are you two okay?'

I need not have asked as their smiling, dirt-streaked faces and peals of giggles told me what I needed to know. Checking each of them over quickly to make sure there weren't any unreported injuries, I then wrapped the two of them in my arms.

'I think this is a good time to take a break and have some lunch. What do you two think?' I asked.

'Yes!' they both shouted, clapping their hands. 'But, Mommy,' Margaret said, trying to look serious, 'I hope you're not going to give us soup.'

Laughing, I scooped the two of them up and carried the giggling bundle of little-girl silliness into the house. Glancing out the kitchen window while I prepared lunch a few minutes later, I smiled at the garden with its neat rows of plantings, Hannah's stone angel, and the girls' garden-soup hole at one end. I realized then, that the real magic of gardening wasn't contained in any books. While it was true that to garden was to establish a relationship with the turning of the Earth, the waxing and waning of the moon, and the subtle shifts between seasons, what mattered even more to me was that the connection between my life and the Earth was richer and more joyful for having shared it with my girls.

Sunday

I woke slowly in my own bed, feeling dazed and dreamy. A breath of warmth wafted into my nostrils as I inhaled the mossy, musky scent of Roger, still lingering on my skin. Closing my eyes, I ran my hands over my body, recalling the touch of his fingers as I drifted through my memories of the night before.

I had felt my heart, petal-by-petal, gently opening. I had been both in my body and outside it as he entered me, as we stared into each other, eyes wide open. 'We are there,' he had whispered, his eyes filling with tears. Later, he had unwound his body from our embrace and, kneeling at the foot of the bed, pressed his hands together in a posture of prayer, then lifted and kissed my feet.

I had felt nothing uncertain or shameful in that place. Fully awake to myself, aware of every movement in my body, I had surrendered everything – all my regrets, pain, unfinished business, faults and dreams – and felt my self-imposed boundaries, like the sides of a box, fall away. Without shame or regret, I felt myself and allowed myself to be seen truly naked. I knew that in that moment of ultimate vulnerability, I had become both his and mine.

Rising slowly from the bed, I felt a new awareness in my body. Every movement, even reaching for the glass of water on the table beside me, felt deliberate and measured. Standing in the shower, I inhaled the soap's lavender scent and felt my muscles softening as the warm water coursed over my body. Towelling myself dry, I stared at my face in the mirror, half expecting to see another, more experienced, knowing woman there, but was relieved to see that the eyes looking into mine were the ones I had always seen.

Once dressed, I went downstairs to the kitchen, opened the door and stepped outside. The light, the birds and the waving grass – the outline of everything was sharper to my eye. Walking through the meadow to the end of the path, I realized why everything looked different to me now. For the first time in my life, I knew that love was not something exclusive or attached to one person or idea. It was the experience of being wholly and completely one's self, without boundaries or hesitation. And in that, because of that, everything and everyone else could be truly seen.

I had just returned to my room and opened my journal when I heard a knock on my door. Opening it, I saw Roger standing there, all smiles and blowing kisses, still sweaty from his morning run.

'Good morning,' he said, bouncing excitedly from one foot to the other. 'What were you planning to do on this perfectly lovely day?'

'I was thinking of taking a long walk to Thoreau, the cabin

in the woods,' I said, smiling. 'Although it *is* my own, secret hideaway, I'd love to share it with you.'

'I'd like that very much,' he said, his eyes twinkling mischievously.

Playfully, he grabbed me around my waist and lifted me off the floor, twirling me in circles as if we were ice-dancing partners. Throwing my head back, relaxing in his arms, I felt positively delicate in my long, tall body. Lowering me to the floor, he grabbed my shoulders and pulled me close for a long kiss.

'Good. That's settled then,' he said, breaking away. 'I'm going to take a quick shower. Let's meet in half an hour in my room.'

I returned my journal to the desk drawer, picked up my backpack, and went down to the kitchen to make a couple of sandwiches for our lunch. Returning up the two flights of stairs to Roger's room, I knocked on the door and entered. I could hear the shower running in the bathroom. I set my backpack on the sofa and wandered around the room, looking more closely at Roger's life, at Roger's things.

I tried to imagine what it might be like for us to live together – waking to his embrace, listening to the sound of him getting ready in the bathroom each morning, seeing our clothes tumbled together in the laundry basket at the foot of the bed. I realized that I couldn't quite imagine any of it actually happening – not so much because I didn't think it would, but because I was now so engaged and interested in my own life, that I had no need to imagine a life more alive and real than this one I was just getting to know.

I lay in Roger's arms on the cabin's twin bed, watching the afternoon shadows move along the wall, listening to the frogs calling from the pond down the hill and the sound of his breath while he slept. Roger loved everything about the tiny space, just as I had known he would. Seeing his genuine enthusiasm for a place I loved so much, I was reminded that the connection between us wasn't based on where and how we had lived; the two of us shared similar perspectives about what mattered and spoke the language of a world that, until now, I had thought was mine alone.

The two of us had arrived just after noon, in time to eat lunch together on the steps of the front porch. At one point during our meal, a beautiful blue dragonfly had landed on the edge of Roger's plate.

'Oh, look,' he exclaimed in a hushed voice. The two of us marvelled at the insect's oily iridescence, watched his long tail twitching, and his filmy, see-through wings fluttering in the breeze. 'Dragonflies were my first introduction to beauty,' Roger said quietly. 'I still remember when I saw one for the first time. I must have been three or four.'

Looking at Roger while he spoke, I could almost imagine what he must have looked like then. He would have had more hair, of course, perhaps a tumble of blonde curls, the same light blue eyes and thick, strong legs. I had no doubt his mother had her hands full following him around as he explored the world, picking up everything and looking at it closely, before dropping it and scampering to the next thing.

After lunch, I took him on a short tour in and around the cabin, refilled the mug on the table with more fresh flowers, and then the two of us had fallen into bed. Now, careful not to disturb him, I disentangled myself from his sleepy embrace. Slipping my feet into my sandals, I opened the screen door, stepped through and then eased it closed. The air was hushed and humid. Tiny bugs buzzed around my head and face as I followed the path from the cabin to the main trail. Picking my way carefully through the leaves and prickly branches, I paused every once in awhile to wipe drops of sweat from my face.

Ahead, through the trees, I saw the reason for my foray. The index cards, now wind-whipped and soggy, were still tacked to the trees. I had noticed them earlier as Roger and I passed, but had decided not to retrieve them then. This was necessarily a solitary task. Approaching, I saw that the ink had smeared into unintelligible blue markings and then, in the warmth of the sun, dried. Removing them from the tree, I put the tacks in my pocket, then ripped the cards into tiny pieces and put them in my pockets too.

Walking slowly back towards the cabin, I fingered the pieces of paper. They seemed to me now so many pieces of unlived dreams no longer needed. I was already lifetimes away from those hours spent in loneliness and longing, just one day before.

Peeking Behind the Curtain

I was curled up in the wing chair next to the fireplace in our living room, lost in a book about reincarnation, while a thin ribbon of smoke from a stick of incense filled the air with its musky scent.

In the distance, as if from another world, I could hear the thump, thump, thump of Will and his friends dribbling a basketball in the driveway outside, and Margaret and Madelaine giggling as they played Barbie dolls in their room upstairs. Although Claude was due home any minute from work, and the whole house was strewn with toys, pieces of board games abandoned halfway through, and the remains of the girls' picnic lunch, I was too engrossed in my book to feel concerned. These days, I wasn't waiting for the answers to come to me; I was doing everything I could to get God's attention.

A small group of friends had recently started meeting at my house on Friday mornings to read and discuss books on topics ranging from dream interpretation to psychic phenomena to the inherent wisdom of other spiritual traditions. While my orientation to God and life had always felt particularly Christian, I also was instinctively drawn to the more mystical aspects of other religions. The idea of reincarnation, for example, particularly appealed to me, not only because it offered a reason and context for Hannah's life and death that was comforting and made sense, but also because I had sometimes felt an unexplainable relationship with other people and times that the understanding of reincarnation helped explain for me.

Friday Morning Spiritual Group, as we called it, offered me an opportunity to converse with a community of similarly curious women who, like me, were living mostly conventional lives as wives and at-home moms. Where I had once met with friends to drink coffee and talk about our lives and kids, I was now drinking coffee and talking about God and the nature of reality. I was feeling less and less like a weirdo trying to fit into a more traditional world, and more like the young woman I had once been who frequently wandered into other people's churches in the middle of the week to light a candle, sit in silence and pray.

Suddenly, the sound of Claude's heavy footfalls on the steps catapulted me out of my reverie. Seeing me, he picked his way through the debris strewn across the living room and came to a stop in front of me. My eyes, having been focused so long on the printed page, took a moment to refocus.

'What's for dinner,' Claude said, his face darkening.

'I don't know yet,' I said, 'I got lost in this great book I'm reading.'

Claude glanced at the title, Many Lives, Many Masters.

'You're crazy,' he said, disgusted. 'All this hocus-pocus incense and reincarnation shit. And I'm sick of all those crazy friends of yours hanging out here too.' Turning on his heel, he stomped up the steps to our room. Closing the book, I smiled.

These days, feeling more confident and sure of who I was becoming, I no longer felt the sting of Claude's criticism in the same way. I understood that his biting words and resentment of the friendships and interests I was developing outside our relationship were symptoms of his need to keep me close to home. And I refused any longer to allow his threats or anger to clip my wings.

Ocean of Love

The sun was warm on my face as I watched Will body surf on the waves of the incoming tide while Margaret poked tattered seagull feathers into the turrets of a sandcastle and Madelaine buried my feet in the sand. The beach was deserted except for the four of us and an elderly man who was trolling for treasure with a metal detector. I loved coming to the ocean. The endless horizon and relentless waves never failed to open me to a bigger perspective on my life, and there was something wild and precise about the slope of dunes whose dips and crests had been cut into the sand by fierce winds.

Smiling at Madelaine, I began to wiggle my toes underneath the mound she had built. We started giggling as soon as the tips of my toes broke through. Quickly, she dumped small handfuls of sand on top of my feet, but to no avail.

'Come here, Margaret,' she called out above the sound of the waves, 'Mommy's feet are trying to get away!'

Margaret jumped up, grinning, and started running towards us. 'Don't worry, Maddy, I'm coming,' she said.

Dropping onto the sand next to Madelaine, the two of them began scooping mounds on top of my legs. Now all three of us were laughing as no matter how much sand they piled on top of me, my toes kept wiggling through. Will, catching a glimpse of the commotion, splashed his way out of the water.

'Help us, Willy,' Margaret and Madelaine called out in unison. Will, glancing at me to make sure it was okay, laid down on the sand. Digging his feet in, he used his arms like the jaws of a front loader and shoved a giant mound of sand onto my feet, completely burying the girls' feet too.

'Grrr,' I growled, grabbing at Margaret and Madelaine, who squealed and landed in my arms. Not wanting to leave Will out, I heaved my legs out of the sand and, using them like scissors, trapped him too. The four of us fell into each other, laughing and tickling each other. Breathless and beaming, I gradually extracted myself from the pile and gave each of them a kiss. Watching the three of them play together, I savoured the simple and beautiful connection I felt with them, which was unique to the way I felt in the company of anyone else.

As a mother, I always had loved my children unconditionally, but as a wife, I still longed for a deeper, more trusting intimacy than I had known with Claude. Staring past the ocean's horizon, I knew that, as far as my marriage was concerned, I had been hanging on for too long to the edge of a sinking boat. But beneath that knowledge there lurked an unspoken fear. What if the problems between us were more mine than his, and I was incapable of being in a healthy relationship with a man?

Monday

FOR THE FIRST TIME SINCE I HAD ARRIVED, I OPENED THE DOOR
to my minivan and climbed in. I had decided that I would
head into town to buy a goodbye card for Roger and a copy
of his most recently published book. I also suspected it might
be good for me to venture into the outside world to re-accli-
matize for a short time.

Turning the key in the ignition, I glanced around at the
assortment of Happy Meal toys, baby wipes and Nintendo
Game Boy magazines littering the floor. Sniffing the air, I
detected a not-so-familiar odour that I quickly identified as
coming from a crumpled-up fast food bag one of the kids
had stuffed under a back seat. I left the engine running and
carried the offending bag to a garbage can outside the barn.
The poignancy of the moment did not escape me: after a
week of freshly grown produce from the garden, I wanted
nothing to do with fast food.

Climbing back into the minivan, I smiled at the tumble of
toys and books, savouring the thought that tomorrow I
would be able to see and hold my kids. No matter how much

the time away had nourished me, I knew that being separated from them for so long had only been bearable because I truly believed it would enable me to be a more patient, trusting and joyful mother. Now I felt more certain than ever that I could no longer allow the toxicity of Claude's and my unhappiness with our lives and each other to contaminate our family.

Easing the car out onto the road, I drove along the highway much more slowly than usual, content to stay in the right lane while others raced by. I knew that my decreased appetite for speed and fast food was only a taste of what lay ahead. Without question, Claude's dream of returning to the way things had been before Hannah got sick was something I could not share. I had seen too much about what else was possible for me and for my life. While Claude had taken the first step by refusing to wear his wedding ring, it was I who would have to make the final break. I knew I would have to re-constellate the whole of my life in order to bring this same sense of love and possibility to my kids.

In the flickering candlelight, I ran my fingers along the dips and curves of Roger's body and along the ridge of a scar on his hip. I inhaled the scent of him deep into my lungs and prayed that his gaze might be imprinted forever in the darkness behind my eyes. The whisper of hope that we might see each other again was weighted down with the more real possibility that we would not. Our love, though, seemed bigger than any uncertainty about what might or might not happen; its blessing, an unspeakable promise.

Earlier, the two of us had shared our last evening meal at an Italian restaurant in town. After four glasses of chilled Pinot Grigio between us, as the waiter brought baskets of bread, plates of salad and pasta, coffee and dessert, Roger and I alternated between gazing deeply into each other's eyes and doubling over with laughter as he began speaking everything with a ridiculously exaggerated, thick, Italian accent.

I felt the luckiest woman in the world, knowing I had loved and was still loving such a good and handsome man. Being with him, I felt like a more beautiful version of myself. And I was thankful that, when packing for the retreat, I had added at the last minute my favourite turquoise-coloured summer dress, a pair of dangly pearl earrings, and black, strappy sandals. At the end of our meal, while we waited for the waiter to prepare the bill, I pulled a copy of Roger's book, *Sacred Journeys in a Modern World*, from my purse and shyly handed it to him.

'I'd love for you to inscribe it,' I said. Roger took the book from me, perched his eyeglasses on the end of his nose, and removed his pen from his eyeglass case. Staring thoughtfully into space for a long moment, he then turned towards me and said, 'If you don't mind, I'd like to keep this for a while and give my inscription some thought. Under the circumstances, I want it to be true and circumspect, at the same time.'

Now, enjoying the warmth and solidity of Roger's embrace, in the flickering light of his room, I felt more aware than ever of the incredible, impossible circumstance we were in. Although it seemed crazy, it also felt right that there had been no talk of exchanging addresses or phone numbers, and, as far as I knew, neither of us expected to either. As much as I loved and appreciated the time we had together, for almost 16 years I had been a satellite, orbiting around one man; the last thing I wanted was to leave one constellation simply to orbit around another.

Instead, I felt certain that it was time for me to create a new container for the simpler, more creative and less angry life I knew I wanted to share with my kids. And I also trusted that, once we had settled into this new life, I might consider touching in again with Roger. After all, I had learned enough in the past 10 days not to leave everything to fate; I had seen his e-mail address earlier in the week and was sure it was one I would remember.

Peeling the Skin Off a Snake

I sat in the dark of the quiet house, staring at the blank page in front of me. For almost a month, I had been trying to begin the book I wanted to write about Hannah and her life, believing it might be the answer to the restlessness I was feeling. But after all this time, I had only managed to get three days of the story down. Sitting at the dining room table now, I realized that however much I wanted to write it, right now I couldn't.

Instead, I pulled my journal in front of me and began to pour out all the words I dared not say aloud to Claude or anyone else onto the page. My life had always seemed more understandable, more manageable, when I was able to articulate my feelings in writing. Even so, as I reread the words I had just written in my journal and stared at the moon in the window, searching for more, I felt that writing and publishing a book would have to happen in some other lifetime than the one I was living, my time and attention was already so stretched.

Any hope I felt for my future now came from knowing that the 10-day retreat my sister had arranged for me to take was on the horizon. I was scheduled to drive to Michigan with my kids in early July, less than a month from now. Already, it was feeling like a door had been opened for me, just ahead, and in no time at all, I would know what was on the other side. Until then, I felt as if I were simply clinging to the coat-tails of God.

Closing my journal, I stood up from the dining room table and carried my mug into the kitchen, rinsed it out and laid it on the top shelf of the dishwasher. The last of the embers had almost burned down in the fireplace, as I walked through the downstairs, making sure the windows were closed and doors were locked. Pausing in front of the refrigerator, I stared for a moment at the finger paintings Margaret and Madelaine had made in pre-school. In one, a painting of our family, Claude, Will, Margaret, Madelaine and I were smiling and holding hands, while Hannah, as an angel with a sparkly halo, hovered above us.

Before turning off the last living room light, I caught a glimpse of my reflection in the picture window. It was as if I were suddenly on the outside of my self and my life, looking in. I saw my face, tired but young, my tall, thin form, well-dressed, surrounded by the furnishings and accoutrements of a comfortable life. I suddenly felt ashamed to be so ungrateful and restless in a story that so many others, even I from the outside looking in, could see was a blessed thing. Climbing the steps to the kids' rooms, I stood for a while in each doorway, watching them sleep. Their faces were so peaceful in the moonlight. Whatever hell Claude and I had been putting them through, there was no sign of it now. Perhaps it still wasn't too late for them, for us, to find another way to make things work.

Sliding into bed, beside Claude's sleeping form, I realized that by pouring so much time and attention into trying to figure out what I was supposed to be doing with my life, I had been peeling the skin off the snake, rather than waiting for it to shed itself. I understood now that the real challenge facing me wasn't about willing myself into another life, but rather being grateful for the life I already had.

A Man Holding on to a Woman Letting Go

The sun was melting behind the hills into pools of gold and orange. I switched the car's headlights on and reached for the cell phone. Not knowing whether the retreat centre where I would be staying for the next ten days had a phone or not, I decided to check in with Claude while I could. My heart raced with anticipation as I listened to the ring of the phone in my ear and prayed he would answer. The two of us hadn't spoken since our strained goodbyes in the driveway a few days before, but my body had already forgotten about the hurt between us. I couldn't wait to tell Claude that despite the difficulties we'd experienced in our marriage in the past years, I had not forgotten how much I still loved him.

'Hello,' Claude answered.

'Hello, Claude. It's me,' I said, my heart leaping in my chest.

'Oh, I'm so glad you called,' he replied quietly. 'I've been thinking about a lot of things since you left, and there's something I need to say.'

I smiled, imagining that this was the scene in the movie of my life where everything was going to be made right. The pain we had been tossing back and forth was about to melt away. Claude was going to tell me he loved me and missed me and would do anything if I would only hurry back home. And I would tell him I loved him too, and that because of the strength of our love, everything was possible between us.

Claude was silent on the other end of the phone. I realized I was holding my breath.

'First, I really want our marriage to work. I'm willing to compromise on everything we've discussed with the marriage counsellor,

except I do need to have more sex. The other thing,' he continued, 'is that I found your journals and I've been reading them. There are a few entries I want to read out loud to you now, and when I'm finished, I want you to explain why you wrote what you did.'

There was a crackling noise on the line, as the connection began to break up. I heard Claude's voice as he began to read my own words to me. I pictured my journals where I had left them, safely tucked away in my underwear drawer, and remembered the pain I had poured onto their pages. Claude's voice droned on, but I made out less and less of what he was saying as the static on the line became louder and more disruptive. My fingers gripped the steering wheel. I felt my breath rising and falling in my chest. I was aware of the beating of my heart and was surprised by how measured and calm it was.

I knew that any other time in my life I would have felt a thousand other things in a moment like this – outrage, violation, shock, despair – but instead, untouched by Claude's words or actions, I felt nothing but a deep sense of love and compassion for him.

A certainty – strong and separate from this man and his needs – began to pour through me. I finally understood, in the quietest place inside, that no matter how much I loved Claude, I could no longer feel responsible for his happiness, just as I could not make him responsible for mine. Happiness, contentment, and love were not experiences we could give each other; they were simply experiences we could share or be. It was as if I had been toting a bubble of compromises, sacrifices, and submission around with me for the whole of our relationship, believing that if I were to try harder, be more loving, do more, that both of us would finally be happy. And in this single moment it had released its hold and, like a balloon, floated up and away from me.

Whatever was going to happen in the days ahead, I knew I was now a million miles away, and I was never going back.

Tuesday

THE WOODS WERE ALMOST SILENT AS I MADE MY WAY TOWARDS the cabin in the early morning light, stopping and bending down now and then to pick handfuls of tiny purple and yellow flowers that lined the path. I had decided, on waking, to spend the first few hours of my last day rocking on Thoreau's front porch. It seemed necessary that I return one last time to the place where my life had awakened to itself, especially since it was likely that I might never see it again.

Rounding the bend, I saw dawn spread out like a baby's blanket in the sky beyond the trees and the edge of the cabin's pitched roof. A chubby brown woodchuck was nosing his way through clumps of grass in the front yard, while several jays, perched on surrounding branches, warned each other of my unannounced arrival. My pace slowed as I gazed at the way the lace-curtained windows of the cabin seemed to watch my approach, and even the porch's rocking chair appeared to be anticipating my company as it rocked back and forth in the breeze.

I encouraged my mind to take as much time as it needed

to imprint the image before me, and promised my heart that I would never forget the woman I had become in the graceful footprint of this place.

My hand was shaking as I handed Roger the card in its white envelope and the little blue vase I had filled with wildflowers gathered on my walk through the woods. The two of us stood almost awkwardly in front of each other. It was still fairly early, and Roger's eyes looked sleepy, as if he had just rolled out of bed. My heart was such a tumble of emotions, I was afraid to speak, not knowing what I might say.

'Thank you, Maria,' Roger said quietly, and then handed me the copy of his book. I swallowed hard, trying to hang on to my composure, and nodded. Two fat tears rolled down and dropped off my chin.

'Aren't you going to read what I wrote?' he asked. I shook my head, having decided in advance not to read his inscription while we were still together. I wanted to be able to trace the scrawl of his words to me when he was no longer within reach of my kiss.

Looking into each other's eyes, we were drawn as if by an invisible cord into each other's arms. I willed myself to remember everything about this moment, the strength of his arms around my waist, the salty taste of his lips. Finally, impossibly, we released our grip.

'Beauty, you are the sun,' Roger said softly, caressing my cheek.

Opening the door to my car, I unzipped my suitcase and placed Roger's book on top of the other special remembrances I had packed: a single, red rose he had given me, pressed between the pages of my journal, and the t-shirt I had worn the first time we made love, unwashed and still bearing his scent. Turning back to him, I smiled and blew him one more kiss, then climbed into the front seat and pulled the door closed.

Edging the minivan slowly down the dirt drive, I glanced in my rear-view mirror and saw Roger, standing with his arms outstretched, head tipped back, reaching in reverence towards the sky. I realized, then, that his presence in my life had planted a blessing in my heart, that could only take root and spread. Knowing this, I could say goodbye and move into the rest of my life. His love, like everyone else's I had known in my life – my parents and siblings, closest friends, Claude, and especially my kids – was an integral part of who I was, and no matter where I ended up, his love and all the other love I had known in my life would be there.

Whatever Happened to Her?

What Ever Happened to...

A New Life

The moon cast its silvery light over everything as Claude and I held hands and walked. The low murmur of our conversation strung between us in the thick humidity of the August night, and played against the rhythm of our footfalls and the backdrop of the grasshopper's thrum. I mostly stared ahead, as the two of us walked, but once in a while, glancing up, I could see moments in the lives of our neighbours, lit and framed in the windows of their houses.

These days, it seemed Claude and I were having only one conversation, which had started almost a month earlier when the kids and I had returned from Michigan, and I had told Claude I wanted a divorce. I was not prepared for Claude's response. Rather than being angry or relieved, he had been stunned. The next morning, I had watched quietly from the door of our room as Claude lifted his wedding ring from its spot on his dresser and put it on his finger for the first time in eight months. I could feel it now, pressed against the skin of my fingers, as the two of us held hands.

For the first time in our relationship, even more than

when Hannah was sick, Claude and I were being truly honest with each other about who we were and what we wanted for our lives. After so many years of struggling to stay married, it seemed unbelievable that things between us felt so calm. It was as if all this time our fight had been less with each other and more against the inevitability of our divorce. Now, the decision having been made, the relief was both understandable and unavoidable.

As I began to understand and trust what was happening between us, I had told Claude not only about the realizations I had come to in my time away about myself and my life, but also the truth about the extent of my relationship with Roger. While I knew the disclosure would be painful for both of us, I believed that Claude deserved to know, to have his suspicions confirmed. I also wanted and needed to assume full responsibility for my actions, including the consequences of them.

Once again, I had been shocked by Claude's response. While he had expressed his deep pain in having been betrayed, he had also opened his heart to me and shared the details of a relationship he had been too ashamed to tell me about many years before. It seemed, in the 18 years since we had met, there had been significant shifts in both of us internally, but after all the counselling sessions and date nights, the extent of our growing differences had never been honestly or fully explored. The biggest difference between us now was that while Claude continued to hold out hope that our relationship might be saved in one form or other, I, having made the decision that I needed to divorce, was feeling stronger and clearer in myself everyday.

Now, as the two of us walked around and around the block, while Will, Margaret and Madelaine slept in their beds under a babysitter's watchful eye, I felt as close as ever to Claude, but now more as a brother or a friend. Our shared love for our children was still a strong, pure connection between us, and I felt certain that because of that and because of the way our hearts had finally opened up to each other, there was hope we might now be able to create happier lives as individuals and a more respectful and supportive relationship as divorced parents.

Gravity

I was rocking back on the legs of my chair, staring at the ceiling, while Claude absently drummed his fingers on the edge of the kitchen table. The two of us had spent the past two hours raising and then shooting down all the custody options we could think of. Now, having reached an impasse, I felt the gravity of our situation begin to settle like lead in the space between us.

For weeks now, we had been trying to decide how to construct our custody arrangement in a way that would address both our children's needs and our individual needs as parents. At first, we had assumed we would do what most divorcing parents do: have the children live with me in our house in Fair Haven during the week and spend weekends and holidays with Claude in a home he would establish close by. But, while the idea of Will, Margaret and Madelaine remaining in the same house, schools and community met our commitment to keeping their everyday lives as stable and predictable as possible, the customary arrangement didn't support our individual needs as single parents.

Claude wanted everything about his life – his job, his home town, his church – to remain the same, but I felt less certain. While the prospect of being independent for the first time in my life was both terrifying and exhilarating, because I knew so little about what lay ahead, I felt unprepared to support myself financially, much less our children. I had been out of the corporate world for almost 10 years, so the idea of me just slipping back into it seemed unrealistic. Besides, what I really wanted was to explore the possibility of finally writing a book about Hannah's life and death. But the real sticking point, was that Claude kept insisting he wanted to see our children every day, or at least be permitted to stop by to tuck them in every night. No matter which way I looked at it, it seemed a bad idea.

Suddenly, Claude sat straight up in his chair. I glanced at him, feeling the shift in his energy. His eyes as serious as I had ever seen them, Claude turned to me. 'Would you consider reversing the usual way of doing it? I'll stay here, in the house with the kids, as the primary custodian, and you can get a place of your own just down the road.'

I felt as if the life was being squeezed out of my heart.

'Are you crazy?' I shouted, jumping up from the table. Part of me couldn't believe he was serious, although the look in his eyes assured me he was. Turning away, I ran up the stairs to our room, taking two steps at a time, feeling I couldn't get far enough away from the words that had fallen from Claude's mouth. Throwing myself on the bed, sobbing into my pillow, I took several deep breaths, trying to restore a sense of order in my frantic mind. I felt shocked and angry at

Claude for having suggested such an impossible thing, and suspected that underneath he was trying to trap or manipulate me. The first thing to do was to phone my lawyer. I was willing to entertain a lot of new possibilities in my life, but I would never let anyone take my kids.

Release

I lay in bed with my eyes open, staring at the dark ceiling. The house was quiet except for the sound of Claude's snores and the occasional skitter of a squirrel on the roof above. I sat up, readjusted the bulk of my pillow and peered at the luminous green hands of the clock on the dresser. It was an hour after midnight. I lay back and closed my eyes one more time, willing myself to sleep.

It had been almost a week since Claude had first made his suggestion about retaining primary custody of our children. Although I still felt far from ready to agree to his suggestion, I had a lot more information about how it might work and what it might mean. My lawyer had been the first to reassure me that there was no need to panic, explaining in detail the legal ramifications of such an agreement. It seemed that primary custody in our case didn't have anything to do with which parent was more fit or loving, but rather who the children would be with more days of the year. As long as I retained joint legal custody, which Claude and I had agreed I would do, I would not be 'giving up' my kids.

Intellectually, as Claude and I began to discuss the details further, I could see how his proposal might make sense. While he and I had, for years, co-created the illusion that he was incapable of handling anything to do with the house or the kids for more than a few hours, in truth, I knew he was as capable a parent and householder as I was. With his proposed arrangement and the help of a live-in au pair, he would retain the more traditional home environment, work and routine he valued, while I would be able to create a home and career more supportive of the simpler life I now knew I wanted to share with my kids. Claude's plan also eliminated the need for us to sell the house Hannah had died in – something neither of us wanted to do. More important was the fact that Will, Margaret and Madelaine would be able to stay where they were, affording them a sense of continuity that seemed especially important now.

Even so, as my body began to release into sleep, a nameless fear lurked beneath any rational argument I might make. Just before dropping into the dark behind my eyes, I felt a single question float to the surface.

'What am I afraid of?' I asked. Suddenly, my eyes flew open, and I sat bolt upright in bed. In an instant, the source of my fear had come clear. The reason I was hesitating to say 'yes' to Claude's proposal wasn't because I was afraid of losing my children's love or because I felt it would mean I was an incompetent mother. The real reason was that I was afraid of what other people would think.

Having seen the source of my resistance to Claude's plan with such clarity, I finally knew what I had to do. No matter how much I wanted to feel loved and respected by my close friends and community, my family's needs were more important. Trusting what I knew as love, I would agree to visitation with my children on weekends, holidays and summers, and give primary custody to Claude.

Wings, Lifting

Will and I were locked and double-locked into a side-by-side harness, as we grinned and gave the Daredevil Dive operator the 'thumbs up'. I pulled on the buckles of Will's harness once more, just to be sure, then smiled and waved at Claude and the girls who were watching us from behind the ticket-taker's gate.

The night before, Claude and I had broken the news of our impending divorce to Will, Margaret and Madelaine, as age-appropriately as we could. We had all cried. There was no attempt to hide our shared sense of uncertainty and loss. But once the tears had dried, Margaret, having just turned four, and Madelaine, about to turn three, didn't have any questions, while Will had seemed unusually quiet and accepting, as if he had suspected this was coming all along. Now, looking over at him, I felt grateful that Claude had taken the day off so we could take a break from the intensity of what was happening at home, and also give our children a sense that a family was still a family, even when divorced.

'Are you scared, Mom?' Will asked, his eyes bright and

wild as the hoist began to lift us off the ground. I grabbed his hand and held on, knowing it wouldn't prevent us from falling if something went terribly wrong, but wanting to reassure him that he was not alone.

'Not yet,' I said, grinning, 'but I will be when we get to the top!'

As our feet left the asphalt, our bodies pitched forward like birds, arms outstretched as wings, facing the ground. Rows of spectators, lined up along fences on either side, began waving and calling out words of encouragement. I kept my eyes on Claude and the girls, who seemed to be making the most noise. Gradually, as the hoist pulled us higher, the details of the faces of those on the ground began to blur, the sounds of their voices grew fainter, and our eyes became more focused on the spectacular view of the amusement park spreading out below. When I thought we could go no higher, the hoist continued its climb. I felt my heart begin to race like a rabbit in my chest, and looking at Will's face, I saw the first trace of fear in his eyes.

'I think I'm scared now, Mom,' he said, quieter now.

'Yes, Will, I am too,' I replied, knowing that a more honest thing had never been said. 'This is one of those moments in our lives when we're simply going to have to trust that everything is okay. And while we do that, let's also take a moment to appreciate how amazing it is that we are this high, this excited, and this brave together.'

Suddenly, there was a loud, grinding noise as our bodies bounced slightly up and down on the ends of the tethers, our momentum having continued upward even though the operator had halted our climb. Below us, the amusement park was splayed out in bright lights and colours, and far off in the distance I could see a highway, threaded with beads of cars, snaking across green flatland, towards the sea.

'Wow!' Will exclaimed, his fear forgotten now, 'This is so great! Thank you, Mom, for doing this with me.'

'Thank you, Will,' I said, smiling and squeezing his hand.

'Ground control to flyers one and two,' the operator called to us over the loudspeaker, 'when you're ready, pull the cord.'

I turned to Will. 'Do it, Mom,' he said, his eyes full of excitement again. Reaching above my head, I felt for the handle the man had shown me before we left the ground.

'3 … 2 … 1 …' I said aloud, and then pulled as hard as I could on the cord. Even though I had initiated our release, my body was still caught off guard. My stomach lurched into the back of my throat and the skin on my face was stretched back by the air rushing past, my form weightless in free fall. A sound I can only describe as a roar of delight pushed its way out of my chest, as Will and I, still holding hands, felt the straps of the harness catch our fall then lightly bounce back, sending us flying now, swinging out over the cheering crowd and back. I caught a glimpse of Margaret's face as we rushed past, blurred because of our speed, but enough in focus to catch her wide grin.

'Yippee!' Will screamed, waving his arms at the crowd now, 'I'm flying!'

As the arc of our swing began to shorten and slow, I became aware of my breath again, and felt the river of blood coursing through my body. I had never felt so instantly, fully alive. And I could see from Will's reaction, he felt the same way. I knew that this moment I had shared with him was the first of many 'firsts' we were going to experience together and I could only hope that we would both continue to trust life and each other the way we had moments ago in the months and years ahead.

Scarlet Letter

My friend Kim was standing in front of me, her hands on her hips, eyes dark and flashing. 'What makes you think you're so special?' she said. 'Don't you think all of us are tired and bored with our lives at times? We're sticking it out, though. Why can't you?'

The two of us were standing on either side of the island in her newly remodelled kitchen. Her boys and my girls were playing together in the next room. Although I had mentally prepared for the responses I might receive when people first heard the decision Claude and I had made about custody, standing mute in front of Kim, I felt as if I had been struck full-force on the face. More and more, it was beginning to feel as if once again I was in a stare-down between what people wanted for me and what I wanted for myself. I had not realized until now how much courage it takes to show your dreams to someone else.

I had expected people's judgment of me to be harsh and unrelenting, especially since I had decided early on not to deny that I had had a sexual relationship with Roger while on retreat. After all, it hadn't been that long ago when I, too, had believed that adultery was a mortal sin. But I had also hoped that my newfound sense of happiness and peace would at least assuage the doubts of my closest friends. I was wrong. Instead, my friendships, left and right, seemed to be dying slow, painful deaths. I was not only Hester Prynne, unashamedly wearing a scarlet letter, being shut out of a community of people I had come to love and trust. I was Hester Prynne, unashamedly wearing a scarlet letter, who had given up her kids.

Now, facing Kim, I searched my heart for the best words to explain why I still believed everything was okay, to reassure her that Claude and I had made our custody decision *because* we loved our kids.

'Remember the book we all read a few summers ago, *Bridges Over Madison County*, the story of the woman who had the three-day love affair with the dashing, worldly photographer while her husband and children were away?' Kim nodded, her expression grim.

'Well, what happened to me was something like that. In spending so much time on my own and then meeting and loving Roger, I discovered parts of myself that I have always known but had almost forgotten; parts of myself that are alive, beautiful and necessary aspects of the woman I am.'

Kim, glancing at the long, flowing skirt and scarf I had begun wearing now that I was a incense-burning, meditating, pioneer woman, looked sceptical. Boldly, I continued.

'Unlike the woman in the book, though, I do not want to shove the kitchen table on which I once made passionate love into the basement and hide my love letters for my children to find after I'm dead. I truly believe that those I love, especially and most importantly my children, deserve to know the best of who I am and who I am capable of being while I am alive and able to share it with them.' I took a deep breath, trying to gauge Kim's response. She had relaxed her stance, but still looked disapproving.

'Good for you,' she said, 'What about your kids, then. Why can't you do all this and still have them live with you?'

It was a fair question, and I knew it. But I also knew that this was the aspect of the decision I had made that I still found difficult to explain. No matter how I said it, even to myself, it sounded self-centred and short-sighted. But I knew in my heart that my gift in this world was more as an artist than an everyday kind of mother. And my real responsibility to my life, the lives of my children and the world, was for me to have the courage to create a sense of home and work that would allow me time to explore and express the things I wondered about and knew.

But looking into Kim's angry eyes, I didn't have the courage in that moment to say it to her face. Instead, I simply said, 'Even if it isn't obvious to anyone else, I deeply trust that Claude and I are doing what is best for our children and our family. Beyond that, I have nothing to say.'

Kim glared at me, then turned on her heels and stomped into the other room. I expected to feel like crying, but instead, I felt a deep calm settling into my bones. I knew in that moment that people, no matter who they were, were a better judge of their own fears than they could ever be of me.

Apartment by the Sea

Will and Margaret scrambled up the steps ahead of me, while Claude, carrying Madelaine, followed close behind. This was the third apartment we had seen that day. So far, I liked this one best. Three miles from what we were already calling 'Daddy's house', it was situated on a thin peninsula of land, with views of the river and harbour on one side and the expanse of beach and ocean on the other.

'Whoa, Mom, this is a good one,' Will said, having reached the top of the stairs.

'Yes, Mommy, let's get it,' Margaret chimed in, jumping up and down and clapping her hands.

Stepping into the living area, I stopped and turned slowly, taking it all in. The ad in the paper had said the one-bedroom apartment was full of light, furnished, and spacious. I was pleased to see that they were right on all counts. The living room and dining room were one space, flooded with sun from a large window and sliding glass door that framed the views and led to a small terrace. The space was carpeted and furnished with a comfortable blue sleeper sofa, two beige upholstered chairs that folded out into twin-sized beds, a rocking chair, a coffee table, and a rattan and glass-topped dining room set.

I followed Claude into the bedroom. A queen-sized platform bed stood in the centre of the room, flanked by two rows of bookshelves on either side. A large walk-in closet and dresser stood opposite two large windows that overlooked the sea. Crossing the small hall, I peeked my head into the bathroom. Everything seemed perfect, simple, well cared for, and clean. And although it was small, it was beautiful. Already I could picture myself walking the beach every morning, capturing the colours of the sea in paint, writing at the small café table on the terrace, and inviting friends for dinner in the evenings. This place, I knew, could easily be my own, first home, the perfect place for my kids and me.

'What do you think?' I asked Claude, turning and smiling at him.

'I think this is your decision to make,' he replied, more seriously than me. The tone of his voice caught my attention and I paused, staring for a moment into his sad eyes. My heart sank, as I felt how hard this must be for him. So full of my own sense of excitement and anticipation about the changes I was now making in my life, I often forgot how painful it still was for Claude. I had released my hold on the dream we had once shared, but he, it seemed, held on to the hope that things between us were eventually going to ease back towards intimate relationship, with the same hope that had kept him praying for Hannah's recovery until the very last.

Thud

The right indicator was blinking on the car's console as I waited for traffic to clear. Margaret was in the front passenger seat next to me, which was an unusual treat for both of us, since I usually insisted for safety reasons that she and Madelaine ride in the back seat. Today, though, I made an exception as she and I were on our way to have lunch at a restaurant, just the two of us. These days, knowing I would be moving out of the house soon, I was making a specific point to spend time individually with each of the kids.

'Mommy,' Margaret asked quietly, 'am I the reason you and Daddy are getting divorced?'

I forgot all about the traffic on the road in front of me. Pulling the car over onto the shoulder and coming to a stop, I put the emergency flashers on. I reached across the front seat and gathered Margaret into my arms. Burying my face in her hair, I felt tears welling up in my eyes. I had expected and encouraged my children to ask questions of me, but no book or idea could have prepared me for how much it would hurt to see Margaret, at four years old, so wise and yet in so much pain.

'Margaret,' I said with conviction, 'You are definitely *not* the reason Dad and I are getting divorced. And I am so sorry that you even had to wonder about that.'

I felt Margaret's body relax in my arms as she began to sob. Her arms reached around my neck and pulled me closer. She felt so small and vulnerable, cuddled up against me in my lap. Each of my children had a special place in my heart, unique to themselves. Margaret was the baby who had grown in my body in the last year of Hannah's life. It was she I had talked to as I caressed my swollen belly in the middle of the night, in the dark of Hannah's hospital room. Because of Margaret, I had known there was still a reason to hope and live in those impossible months of waiting for Hannah's death.

Now, running my fingers through her hair and kissing the tears from her cheeks, I prayed for strength and wisdom as a mother, wanting more than anything to know that I was truly making the best right decisions not only for me, but also for our family, for my kids.

Mommy Always Comes Back

Tears were streaming down my cheeks as I held Will and then Margaret and Madelaine close enough to my body to imprint their scent on my heart. Gradually, as each of them released their grip, I knew it was time for me to go. Claude hadn't been able to say goodbye. Instead, he had chosen to wait just inside the door of the house. Smiling now through my tears, I encouraged Will, Margaret and Madelaine to join him. I didn't want their last memory of me in that house to be of watching me drive away.

Giving each of them one last hug, I whispered in their ears, 'Remember, I love you, and Mommy always comes back.' All three of them smiled at the reminder.

'We love you, Mommy,' Madelaine said. Will, his eyes close to tears, nodded, as Margaret threw her arms around my legs. 'I love you, Mommy,' she said.

Even though my heart was threatening to break open and bleed all over the driveway, I smiled and waved to the three of them as they went into the house and closed the door. Climbing into the car, I willed my tears to remain inside until I got to the apartment, knowing I would have plenty of time to cry then. As I reversed out of the drive, I glanced quickly into the back seat at the two suitcases of clothes and six boxes of items I had decided to bring with me, including an album of photographs, a blanket of Hannah's and a few drawings she had made, several CDs of favourite music, and my books and journals.

Driving away from everything I loved and knew best, my body felt impossibly heavy, and yet I also felt lighter and free in a way I would have been ashamed to admit out loud. I had taken almost nothing from our home or accounts, wanting my life to be as simple and uncomplicated as possible. And while Claude had offered to cover my expenses for the next month, including my groceries and the cost of a rental car until the divorce was final and the small settlement we had agreed on came through, I hadn't taken a dime more than I thought I might need in order to get back on my feet.

Now, driving alongside the breakwater, I rolled down the window and inhaled the mist blowing in off the shore. Without knowing how anything was going to turn out, good or bad, in the future, I felt relieved, even elated that I was finally and irreversibly committed to the life I had once only dreamed about, a life that now seemed to be dreaming me.

Wish Upon a Star

———

I woke to the warmth of the morning sun pouring through the open window onto my face. Shading my eyes, I sat up in bed, careful not to wake the girls who were sleeping on either side of me. Carefully, I lifted my body from under the covers and swung my feet onto the floor, mindful of Will, who was asleep there on the fold-out mattress.

Padding into the kitchen, I switched the coffee maker on, and made myself a piece of toast. I heard footsteps behind me and turned in time to see Will, in baggy flannel pyjama bottoms, his hair tousled from a good night's sleep, shuffling into the bathroom. Minutes later, as I sipped my coffee and nibbled toast, staring out the window at the spread of sun across the open water, Margaret, followed by Madelaine, came flying into the room, all morning sweetness and giggles, and fell across my lap. Covering them with kisses, I pointed towards the sea.

'How about a morning walk along the beach?' I asked, smiling at Will who was already setting the table for breakfast, pouring milk into bowls of cereal and filling glasses with juice.

'Yes, yes, yes,' all three shouted.

Half an hour later, our pockets stuffed with the gallon-sized bags we used to hold beach treasures, the four of us were trudging across the dunes towards the edge of the water. Our progress was slow as the girls were already bent over, sifting through the sand, scooping up handfuls of shells. As we crested the highest dune and began our descent towards the waves, I caught my breath.

'Look, Mom,' Will exclaimed.

There, spread out across the sand like a mirror image of the night sky, were hundreds and hundreds of starfish, washed up on shore. Margaret and Madelaine ran up to stand beside me and gasped when they saw the beautiful sight. Slowly, the four of us moved closer. I could see now that some of the creatures were still alive, the pointed tips of their bony arms moving over the sand. Two crusty old fishermen, seated in beach chairs behind their fishing poles, saw us approaching.

'Never saw anything like it,' one of them said.

I wanted to kneel in front of the miraculous happening and cry for the bittersweetness of so much beauty and death in one breath. I watched as the girls and Will began to step carefully through the starry expanse. Finally, unable to contain her curiosity, Margaret carefully lifted one of the lifeless forms, running one finger over its rippled edges and studying its underside.

'Oh, Mommy,' she cried, 'It's so sad. I think it's dead.' Lowering the starfish into the water, she crouched on her heels, carefully watching for signs of movement. After a minute or so, she lifted it back. Madelaine, standing quietly behind her, turned to me.

'Mommy, can we take the dead ones home and put them in the bathtub? We have to try to save them,' she said.

I looked at Will, who was already running down the beach, tossing the starfish that were still alive back into the sea. Nodding my head 'yes', I was reminded of the way my children had always been my best teachers, and I felt blessed to be able to witness a sense of hope and possibility as innocent and beautiful as theirs.

Returning

I stepped out of the shower and stared at my image in the mirror. I knew that the woman looking back at me was the same woman who had brought four children into the world, had held Hannah's dying body in her arms, and had loved more than one man. She was also now a woman living on her own, sharing her life with her children on weekends, holding a world of possibilities in her hands.

Reaching for the bottle of Eternity by Calvin Klein that now sat on the edge of my bathroom sink, I smiled, thinking of Roger as I dabbed it on. Days before, I had made a special trip to the mall to purchase this reminder of him. Now, inhaling its scent, I wondered if the changes I had made since we had last been together, if my new independence and confidence, would be obvious to him. Loosening the towel wrapped around my body, I allowed it to drop to the floor. As I stared at my nakedness in the mirror and saw all the ways in which I was not getting younger, I decided it was time to e-mail him.

Tremors

I was sitting in a patch of autumn sun halfway up a rise in the park lawn, just across the path from the Boathouse in Central Park, the place where Roger and I had agreed to meet. I was already trembling with anticipation, wondering what it was going to be like to see him, to be with him, for the first time in the everyday world.

I scanned the crowds of people pouring by, mothers and fathers pushing babies in strollers, kids on roller blades, streamlined bicyclists and the occasional jogger. Suddenly, I saw him, strolling at a leisurely pace towards the Boathouse gate, wearing white linen trousers and a bright blue, long-sleeved shirt. My legs felt too weak to stand. I watched as he stopped at the entrance to the restaurant and glanced around. Seeing him check his watch, I remembered its large round face, black Roman numerals, and well-worn tan leather band.

I knew I couldn't make him wait forever, but I was struggling to catch my breath. My eyes were glued to him and, finally, I took a deep breath and stood. Steadying myself, I walked towards him. I was three paces away when he saw me.

'Hello, Maria,' he said, opening his arms. I could not speak. My eyes full of tears, I felt his arms encircle my trembling body, coming to rest in the small of my back, pulling me close. My head on his shoulder, he held me there, until finally I turned my face to his and kissed his lips. His kiss tasted just as I remembered. I had never felt so close to magic as I did now.

Taking my hand, Roger led me along the path, the way he had come. I felt steadier on my feet now and my head had cleared. Suddenly, Roger stopped and turned towards me. He gazed into my eyes, opening and closing his mouth as if he were trying to say something, but couldn't find the words. Finally he spoke.

'Who *are* you?' he asked. As I gazed back at him, smiling, my answer rose from the centre of my heart, as clear as his eyes and as true.

'I am the second half of your life,' I said.

California

The Pacific Ocean was spread out before me, an endless expanse of lapis blue. From our vantage point on the top of Mount Tamalpais, Roger and I could see San Francisco, a city of white nestled into the bay and the Golden Gate Bridge, its red supports jutting skyward, strung like a necklace with cables. Behind us and below, majestic redwoods created cathedrals of light and shade, filling the canyon with their pungent, earthy scent.

My life had finally brought me to California. I was scheduled to stay for 12 days. Roger had recently moved into a little tree house, 65 steep steps up a mountain, overlooking a redwood canyon. Although San Francisco was often cloaked in drizzly fog, Larkspur, across the bay, where Roger's house was located, always seemed to be bathed in sun. Having endured 53 years of English grey, Roger was in bliss. It also helped that just down the road there was a lovely Italian café called Rulli's, a casually elegant French restaurant called The Left Bank, and an independent bookstore, Book Passage, which was well-known for the intelligent and thoughtful writers and readers it supported.

'I have to bring my kids here,' I said, turning to Roger. He smiled and squeezed my hand. 'Next summer,' I vowed.

Turning to look eastward, towards the soft, golden hills, I tried to comprehend how vast the space was between where I was standing now and the life I had always known.

Star of Bethlehem

The little Christmas tree, its ball of roots wrapped in burlap and tied with a big red bow, stood in one corner of the living room. Will, Margaret, Madelaine and I had decorated it earlier with a ribbon of tiny white lights and assorted seashells and starfish, which the girls had hung from the branches using loops of white string. A tinfoil Star of Bethlehem was fastened to the uppermost branch, and a modest assortment of packages, wrapped with butcher-block paper, sponge-painted by Madelaine, were arranged underneath. Across the room, the glass-topped dining room table was covered with cookie crumbs, chocolate sprinkles and drips of bright-coloured frosting, and in the kitchen, Margaret and Madelaine were rolling out and cutting more sugar cookies, while Will kept an eye on those already baking.

I stood in the centre of the room and smiled. In little more than three months, it seemed that the kids and I had finally settled into the rhythm of this new life. While it hadn't been easy for any of us getting used to being separated from each other for days, when we were together there was a palpable sense of ease and simplicity between us that was all the more sweet because of the spaces in between.

'As soon as you three are finished in there, I'll make some hot chocolate to go with those cookies while you put on your pyjamas,' I said

'Okay, Mom,' the three of them replied in unison.

An hour later, the room dark except for the flickering flame of a candle and the lights on the tree, the four of us were snuggled together on the couch, wrapped in a large down comforter. The room was silent, but in the distance I could hear the rhythmic pounding of the waves on the shore. Glancing at the tumble of bodies laying across my lap, I saw that while Will was still fighting to keep his eyes open, Margaret's and Madelaine's were already closed.

'Mom,' Will whispered, 'this might sound funny, but beside the Christmas when Santa gave me Nintendo 64, I think this might be one of the best Christmases ever.' Reaching for his hand under the comforter, I gave it a squeeze.

'I don't think it sounds funny, Will,' I whispered back. 'In fact, I definitely agree.'

Morocco

It was close to midnight, as I made my way through the airport in Casablanca, Morocco, trying to find the gate for my flight to Marrakech. It wasn't proving to be as easy as I had hoped. None of the signs that I could see were written in English. I thought I might stop and ask for directions, but the only people in sight were men in green uniforms, carrying automatic weapons, patrolling the halls. All of the restaurants and shops along the corridors were closed. Turning a corner, I fell into step alongside a handful of travellers, most wearing robes or business suits, some with headdress, all carrying luggage. Since they seemed to know where they were going, I decided to follow them.

I was scheduled to meet Roger in Marrakech. He had invited me there, along with a small group of friends, to go on a walking journey he was leading in the Sahara desert. I had immediately said 'yes'. The next day, I bought a beautiful leather duffel bag to use as luggage. I felt certain it would make me look more like the seasoned world traveller I had always imagined I would some day become.

Now, though, walking through Casablanca's airport, clutching the bag in my hand, I knew that a cool leather bag does not make a seasoned traveller. I felt particularly conspicuous, a 6 ft 2 in blonde, wearing a long flowered skirt, brown leather boots, and a brown felt cowboy hat I'd ordered from the Boy Scout catalogue. I hoped I didn't look as lost as I felt. Following the others, I saw that we were approaching the first gate that I'd seen which appeared to be open. Airline attendants were scurrying around, checking people in. I handed my ticket to the agent at the counter, assuming that if I were in the wrong place, she would know from my ticket and redirect me. Instead, she barely glanced at it before authoritatively waving me onto the plane.

The flight attendant at the door of the plane smiled at me and pointed me down the centre aisle. It seemed that there was no assigned seating, which wasn't a problem, as there was hardly anyone else on the plane. Spotting a white woman seated on her own, I made my way towards her and sat down. Shoving my bag under the seat in front of me, I turned to her.

'Do you speak English,' I asked.

'Non. Mais je parle francais,' she replied. It had been almost 20 years since I had taken high school French, but I remembered enough to understand what she had said. Smiling at her, I settled back into my seat, and decided the flight attendant's announcement would soon clear things up. The only thing I really wanted to know was if I was on the plane to Marrakech.

I watched as eight more people filed onto the plane and

sat. Finally, the door closed and the flight attendant stood in front and began making announcements on the loud speaker. From what I could gather, she repeated her greeting and safety instructions in three different languages. The problem for me was that none of them were English. As the plane began to taxi away from the gate, I lay my head against the back of my seat and grinned, willing simply to trust that I was on the right plane.

Too excited to sleep, I stared out at the dark sky. Finally, after about an hour, lights appeared on the ground. The plane circled and landed. I stood, put my hat on my head, and gathered my bags. Following the others, I stepped out of the plane and walked along a narrow corridor, which eventually opened into a large, fluorescent-lit waiting area. As soon as I saw Roger, jumping up and down, waving his arms and beaming at me from the other side of the room, I realized that while my life was expanding and opening me to new experiences and places, in truth what I was actually doing was finding my way home.

Scent of a Woman

I was alone in the house, wandering from one room to the next, savouring the integrity and beauty of the life that was being lived by my friend Siobhan, as a woman on her own. Every item in her home had clearly been chosen by Siobhan, or had been given to her by someone who knew her well and had bought the gift with her in mind. There was nothing formulaic or rigid about the way the rooms flowed into each other and the items in them fitted together. What connected every piece of art, ceramic bowl or carved wooden chair was that each piece was imbued with a story from Siobhan's life or travels, and was therefore in relationship, through her, with the whole.

Siobhan and I had met through Roger on the Sahara desert trip. Roger and I were now staying with her, in her home in southern California. Although Siobhan and I were the same age, we had lived very different lives. She owned a successful company in Los Angeles, had travelled the world extensively, and had never had children or married. To me, she was the epitome of what was possible when a woman is unapologetically ambitious about her work and dreams, which was what I was wanting to be.

I just hoped I wasn't too late.

The day before, I had gone with Roger to the Los Angeles Coliseum for the BEA, a National Bookseller's convention. I had intended to get a sense of whether the book I wanted to write about Hannah's life and death was the kind of book that booksellers and publishers might support. Instead, I had left feeling discouraged and overwhelmed. Wandering up and down aisles of publishers' booths, each one featuring too many new books to count, I had almost lost my nerve to write. How could I possibly expect to compete in an industry already filled to capacity with good ideas and excellent writers?

And yet, as I studied the images of Siobhan in the photographs on her mantle, seeing her life unfold through the lens of a camera across different times and places, I saw a woman who had made a life for herself by trusting what she loved most and best. For me, having given myself time in the past year, since leaving Claude, to explore and discover the kind of life I wanted, I knew that writing was what I most wanted to do.

Standing in the middle of the beautiful life and space Siobhan had created, I now knew something else was also true. I was not only going to have to write, I was going to have to do everything I could to make a decent living doing it. I did not want to make a life with Roger or anyone else until I knew I was capable of creating and supporting my self and my children on my own.

River of Healing

I was sitting on the front porch of my parent's house in Traverse City, in the same spot where I used to sit and dream when I was young. Tipping my head back and closing my eyes, I inhaled the sweet, clean scent of the breeze blowing across the surface of Lake Michigan.

My father was sick. Months before, he had been diagnosed with cancer. It was a devastating blow. My father was like a tree that had always lived in the front yard of my life, strong, invincible, protecting. Morality was his measure. He was the reason I had always wanted to do the right thing, to make him proud of me. It was my father who had taught me that I was worthy and beautiful, not because of my sexuality or because I was a woman, but because I was who I was. I could not begin to imagine what my life would be like if he died.

These days, I was feeling less confident, not only because of my father's illness. My divorce from Claude had been finalized more than seven months before, and Claude had decided, once the judge's gavel came down, that he would no longer speak directly to me. Our only communication, at his request, was by e-mail or through the post office. He had rented a post office box for our correspondence, telling me he didn't want anything of mine coming to his house. At first, I had imagined it was only a temporary setback. But I now knew that the only temporary aspect of our relationship had been the ease with which we had negotiated the months before our divorce.

I was also now seriously considering moving to California. Roger had invited me to live with him, in his tree house in the canyon. Although I felt far from ready to marry again, there was such a joy in our being together, and a nourishing sense of spaciousness and support between us that living together felt the next, right step in our relationship. Yet I could not imagine living, even for short periods of time, so far from my kids – any more than I could have previously imagined giving primary custody to Claude. But because Roger had dreamed all his life of living in California, just as I had, I couldn't bring myself to ask him to leave and come to New Jersey.

I felt as if my life were once again sucking me in a direction I would never have chosen for myself, away from the way I had always believed it was supposed to be. And while I trusted the movement because my instincts told me it was right, I also hated it throwing me into the limelight again. Moving to California could only confirm what most people already believed, that I had not only divorced Claude, I had abandoned my kids.

And yet, whatever they believed, I also knew it could not change the truth. Since Claude was now making it

impossible for me to see my children except during scheduled visitation weekends, it would change almost nothing if I
were to live in California during the week and fly back and
forth to New Jersey when I was scheduled to see my kids.
Life on two coasts would also mean that Will, Margaret and
Madelaine would be able to live in California with Roger and
me every summer, which was an idea that appealed to me too.

Sitting now on the stoop of my parents' house, I could
hardly believe how different my life and my children's lives
already were from the childhood memories I had made here.
I felt lucky to be able to return to the home I had grown up
in, to re-immerse myself in the family dynamics that had
shaped my earliest ideas of who I was supposed to be, to see
my mother and father as well as their relationship through
different, more experienced eyes. I understood now that for
most of my life, my goal had been to do what my parents had
done, only better. Now, though, I was beginning to realize
that not only was I not them, I was someone with completely different dreams, wanting to explore a world they, my
parents, had never known.

I heard the screen door behind me open. Turning, I saw my
father, holding two glasses of lemonade, coming towards me.

'Do you mind if I join you, honey,' he asked.

'Not at all, I'd love it,' I said.

Perching on the edge of the stoop, he handed me one of the
glasses. I took a sip, enjoying the tangy sweetness in my mouth
before swallowing. My father cleared his throat. I looked at
him, realizing that he had an ulterior motive in joining me. I
remained silent, wondering what he was going to say.

'Maria, I need to tell you something,' he said finally. My heart leaped into my throat. Suddenly, I was 10 years old again, anticipating a scolding. My father addressed me by my first name only when it was really serious or important.

'I want to talk with you about your life and the decisions you've made and are making.' He cleared his throat again and took another sip of lemonade. My heart was now thudding in my chest. I willed myself to stay focused on my father's words. 'What I have to say,' he continued, 'isn't just about you or your children. It's also about my mother.'

His mother! Although he had always found it painful to speak of her, I knew that my father had loved his mother deeply. For years, he had kept a large, framed photograph of her on top of a table in his office. I could see her image now, in my mind, a dark-haired woman with pale skin, full lips, and deep feeling eyes, wearing a formal-looking, light-coloured suit with a wide-brimmed hat. I knew from what I had overheard as a child that she was a quiet, soft-spoken woman who had been loved by everyone who knew her, and was the wife of a doctor, my father's father, an intense, emotionally abusive, alcoholic man. The source of my father's profound sorrow was that she had died in the hospital of cancer, when my father was 16, before my father and his brothers were even told she was sick.

My father was speaking. 'Honey, I want you to know that, in terms of the decisions you've made in your life this past year, even the difficult one you're considering now, I think you're doing the right thing. It hasn't been easy, I know, to have the kind of courage you've had. But for those of us who love you, and especially Will, Margaret and Madelaine, it is wonderful to see you putting yourself out there. God gives each of us talents to express. Whose right is it to limit the expression of those gifts? I feel lucky to have you as a daughter, and I will always be committed to instilling in you your right to excel.'

I wanted to cry, my heart swelling with gratitude and relief, but my father was not done.

'This has always been a man's world,' he continued. 'And no one knew that more than my mother. But she didn't have the strength to do what you're doing. She put up with a lot of unhappiness and abuse, and it killed her.' He hesitated. I waited.

'What I have to say next might sound strange to most people, but I am sure you will understand. I still feel my mother. Her presence has always been a part of my life. And what I feel in relation to her now is that the decisions you're making as a woman are not only helping you and your children. Your decisions are also healing her.'

I was stunned. I had never heard my father speak like this. As his words sank in, I felt my need to be perfect in his eyes dispersing. I knew then that I had to be willing to endure the disapproval of others in order to be everything I was capable of being. My father had reminded me that not only was I responsible to my own life and the lives of my children, but I was responsible to every women who had come before me and to those who would come after, who needed to be reminded, as I once had, that they are deserving and capable of more.

Where There's Smoke …

The girls were already asleep in the tent. The night sky, stretched over the flat prairie, was dotted with stars. Will and I were savouring the quiet as we took turns poking the smouldering logs of the campfire with sticks. Having already visited the battlefield at Gettysburg, stayed a night in a roadside motel in Illinois, and then continued on to the St Louis Arch, we were now camped by the side of a shallow lake, beneath a willow tree, in the middle of Kansas. Earlier today, after almost a week of travelling, Will had turned to me and asked, 'What day is this anyway?' I knew then that we had finally arrived at the wonderful, magical moment when a vacation truly begins.

The four of us were travelling west to California, our luggage, camping equipment, and coolers of food packed tightly into the trunk of the two-door BMW I had recently purchased – the first car I had ever owned. We had begun our trip with a prayer on the beach in New Jersey. Wading into the Atlantic Ocean, in the same spot where we had gathered starfish months before, each of us had chosen a rock or shell to bring with us, intending to drop them as a greeting into the Pacific as soon as we reached California. Before leaving, we had also stopped at the tree that had been planted in front of our church in Hannah's memory, untied a pink-red heart from its branches, and hung it on our rear-view mirror.

Staring into the licking dance of the fire, I listened to the sounds of the prairie around us: the wind in the willow, the chirping of crickets and the rustling of grass as small (I hoped) animals passed by. Suddenly, Will banged his stick hard on the ground.

'Mom, why did you lie to me?' he asked.

Shocked by the angry tone of his voice and the sudden shift in the air between us, I was temporarily tongue-tied.

'What do you mean, Will,' I managed to say.

'You promised me you and Dad wouldn't get a divorce,' he replied, glaring at me, his eyes filling with tears.

I felt my heart soften, as I studied his face, trying to decide what to say. I could still remember when he was a baby, growing inside me, the way when his heel was digging into my ribs, I simply had to touch him where it hurt and his whole body would gently shift. Now, at 11½ years old, he was a young man, almost taller than me, with my eyes, his dad's lips, and an already broken-open heart. Hannah's death as well as the divorce had shattered his innocence. He knew things about life that no one his age, or perhaps any age, should know.

'I am so sorry, Will,' I began, choosing my words carefully. 'I can't even begin to imagine how painful Dad's and my divorce must feel to you.' I paused, wanting to get the next part exactly right.

'But I don't remember my promise the same way you do.' I saw the shift in his gaze. He was eyeing me suspiciously now. I took a deep breath.

'What I remember promising you is that Dad and I were going to do everything we could to avoid getting divorced. But in the end, we weren't able to work things out.'

Will was silent for a moment, as if he were calculating the differences between his memory and mine in his head. Finally, he nodded.

'Yeah, I guess that is what you said,' he agreed, kicking dirt into the fire with his foot. 'I probably just remembered it the way I *wished* you had said it.' It was my turn to nod in agreement. I waited, allowing him a moment with his thoughts, and then reached out to touch his arm.

'I'm still sorry, though, Will,' I said quietly. 'Divorce is not easy for anyone. Dad and I knew that, which is why we tried so hard for so long to try to make our marriage work. And, whatever Dad and I thought divorce would be like, we had no way of knowing how much it would hurt you and the girls.'

At that, Will's face crumpled, and I took him into my arms. Rocking him back and forth on my lap, just as I had when he was a baby, I held him until his sobs subsided and his body softened.

'I'm sorry I was mad at you, Mom,' he whispered. I smiled and gave him a hug.

'You don't need to apologize for your feelings, Will,' I said. 'I'd much rather have you be honest with me than nice. I'm your mother, and that means that I love you no matter what – no matter what you feel, no matter what you do. What is also important to remember, though, as you begin to make decisions in your life is that over time and with experience your dreams may change, just as what you believe and what you need may change too.'

Holding Will and feeling the words I had just spoken resonating in me, I realized that Will wasn't the only one who needed to be reminded of my message. Having given myself permission to change what I had always believed about my self and my life, I now understood that no matter what I did as a result, staying married or getting divorced, living in New Jersey or moving to California, I was simply exchanging one set of joys and challenges for another. One life was not necessarily better or worse, it was simply different.

Penthouse in Las Vegas

The girls were jumping up and down in the middle of the king-sized bed while Will, already wearing one of the hotel's thick, terry cloth robes, pressed the buttons on the remote control and watched the giant television screen rise out of the credenza in front of him.

'Mom, this is the coolest place EVER!' he exclaimed.

I had to agree, although at this point, almost any place with a bathtub would have excited me. After three days of camping in the Grand Canyon, and more than 2½ weeks on the road, I was ready for some pampering. And this was definitely the right place for that: the penthouse suite at the Mirage Hotel and Casino in Las Vegas. One of Will's requests, when our trip began, was that we stay one night in an extra-fancy hotel. I had explained all of this, including the story of our cross-country trek, to the guy at the front desk. Smiling, he had handed me a special key to the elevator.

'It's a slow day for us,' he said, 'so I'll only charge you $120, the regular room rate. Enjoy.'

Even I hadn't known what to expect when the elevator

doors opened. I'm certain my mouth must have dropped open – the kids' did. Stepping into a cavernous marble foyer, lined with gilt-edged mirrors, and hung with a gigantic crystal chandelier, we dropped our luggage on the floor as the elevator doors silently slid shut behind us. The suite contained a formal living room, a dining room with seating for 10, two bedrooms, and a bathroom almost big enough to hold the whole of Roger's house.

Immediately, the girls had begged to be allowed to swim in the bathtub. It was that big. While the water ran into the marble swimming pool, Margaret uncapped two bottles of bubble bath and poured them in. Within minutes, to the girls' delight, the tub looked like a wedding cake with frothy, white frosting. Meanwhile, Will was running through the place, looking in every closet, pressing every button he could find. Standing at the expanse of floor-to-ceiling windows that lined the whole of one wall, listening to the giggles of the girls in the bath and the blaring noise of the surround-sound television Will was watching, I gazed out at the courtyard of palm trees, tiki bars and swimming pools below and the massive range of mountains in the distance.

I could hardly believe that our journey across the country was almost over. In two days, we were scheduled to arrive in Malibu, to stay a few days with Siobhan and drop our shells and stones from the Atlantic into the Pacific. Then, after a few days in Los Angeles, we would head up the winding coast on Highway One to San Francisco and Roger.

Turning from the window, I strolled across to the bathroom, where the commotion had gotten even louder. As I stepped through the door, I laughed out loud when I saw what the girls were doing. Standing in front of the long stretch of mirrors, the two of them, speaking to each other in exaggerated English accents, were dabbing themselves with white powder puffs they had found in a container on the sink, and rubbing handfuls of lotion all over their bodies.

'Don't we smell pretty, Mommy?' Madelaine asked, turning to smile at me.

'Let's call Dad. I want to tell him about how fancy we are,' Margaret said.

'Okay, no problem,' I said. 'I've seen about seven phones in this place. I'm sure there must be at least one in here.'

Suddenly Madelaine's smile faded and morphed into a pout. 'I miss my Daddy,' she said.

'Oh, baby, of course you do,' I replied, forgetting about the phone for a minute, sweeping her into my arms.

'Divorce is no fun,' Madelaine continued, her voice muffled now as her face was buried in my neck. 'I'm always missing somebody. When I'm with Daddy, I miss you. And when I'm with you, I miss Daddy.'

Will, overhearing Madelaine's words, came and stood in the doorway. Margaret, patting Madelaine's back, said soothingly, 'I know it's hard, Maddy. Sometimes, when parents are divorced, you cry because your mom or dad goes on a trip, or has to go swimming or to the restaurant by themselves. But it's not all sad. Because our Mommy and Daddy are divorced, we now get to have two houses and two bedtimes and lots of adventures. And at night, we don't have to decide which parent gets to read us a story, get us drinks and turn on the hall light.'

Madelaine nodded, raising her head from my shoulder and wiping her eyes. Will came over to her and bent down, stroking her cheek.

'I understand that you feel sad, Maddy,' he said, quietly, 'but as hard as it is for us now that Mom and Dad are divorced, it was much harder for our whole family when they were living together. I know you don't remember, but I do.'

Surprised by his words, and grateful, I turned to him. Will stood up, smiling, and winked at me.

Window Box in the Canyon

I lit the votive candle on my desk, and sat down in the antique oak chair. I was now officially living in California with Roger, and had begun writing a proposal for my book. I already knew the title was *Hannah's Gift*, and that Hannah's favourite red patent leather Mary Janes would have to be on the cover. What I didn't know, was whether I would ever be able to find a publisher willing to publish it, much less pay me any money for it. But while my finances were a reality that desperately needed to be addressed, I wasn't thinking about that now.

My desk was nestled into a windowed nook in our bedroom, with views of the redwoods in the canyon below. With its soft pine top and curved iron legs, it looked writerly and elegant, just as I'd hoped it would. I had a new laptop computer too, and a small silver lamp with a fluted glass shade. In one corner of the desk were a stack of books by some of my favourite poets and writers – Annie Dillard, Mary Oliver, Annie Lamott and Jane Hirshfield – and photographs of Will, Hannah, Margaret and Madelaine in carved silver frames.

These days, everything in my life felt as if it was in support of everything else. Although there were many nights when I cried myself to sleep, missing my kids, Will, Margaret, Madelaine and I still saw each other according to the visitation schedule Claude and I had originally agreed to. And travelling back and forth to New Jersey on weekends, although expensive, was easier than I expected. The four of us spent weekends in a lovely, furnished but unused apartment of a friend on the upper east side of Manhattan. If the New York apartment was not available, we sometimes stayed at a hotel with a pool or with our good friends, the Lores, whose children were the same ages as mine.

Life with Roger was proving to be a graceful one. Our differences, which at one time had intimidated me, now served as fuel for the conversations we loved to have, and as a basis for the life we were making together. In the months since I had moved in, his friends had quickly become ours. Drinking coffee each morning in the café, returning home to write, read, walk in the canyon, or simply think quietly on the deck overlooking the trees, I had quickly acclimatized to a quieter, more thoughtful pace. Evenings were more lively as the two of us almost always went out to dinner at a restaurant, or hosted a gathering at home with friends.

Sitting at my desk, staring at the blinking cursor on my computer screen, I paused. This was always my favourite time of the day, the morning, when every word that was going to emerge in the next few hours hung expectantly in the air. Writing about Hannah was a joy, but it was also a return to the deepest pain I had ever known. The grief I still felt, while familiar now, was a yawning hole in me, like the Grand Canyon. I could only cross it in good weather, at select narrow places, in solitude and with no distractions. As my fingers began to pick their way across the keyboard, I felt a sense of elation, as if I were finally, literally, taking my life in my hands.

Death Valley

The sun's heat was creating shimmering waves on the surface of Death Valley's arid salt flats. My cowboy hat, the same one I had worn in the Sahara, afforded me my only protection, shading my eyes as I walked. Row upon row of mountains receded into the distance in lighter and lighter shades of grey on either side, but the horizon stretched endlessly in front of us.

Rowan, a filmmaker and new friend of mine in California, had teamed up with Simone, a television personality for MTV-Europe to make a documentary of 10 women journeying through the desert. Originally, she had asked Roger to organize it, but as he was already scheduled to be in the Sahara at the same time, he suggested that I lead the trip. Because he and I had already done a similar journey together, with another group of people in Death Valley earlier in the year, I felt up to the task, and excited too. If nothing else, I needed the money. The reserves I had saved from my settlement with Claude were quickly dwindling.

The women and I had set up our base camp three days

before. Each morning, after breakfast, we cleaned up camp, packed lunches and filled our canteens with water, then headed out. Everything was carried out in silence, including the filming, which was being done by an all-woman crew. In the evening, though, after the dinner dishes had been washed and put away, I built a fire in the stone pit. As the sun set behind the mountains, and the dark descended on our camp, opening up the starry night sky, each woman was invited to speak of what she had experienced that day.

It was a particularly poetic and powerful experience for me as I was seeing, with my own eyes, the strength and beauty of what women can accomplish together, when united by a shared intention. I had been particularly moved by the way each of us, without discussing it, had willingly packed and carried extra food, water and medical supplies each morning, just in case. There was a way, too, that the wildness of the land and the intensity of the elements had shorn us of any pretence and fostered a deep sense of trust between us.

Today, walking with the others, my well-worn leather boots leaving prints in the white, salty sand – not unlike those left by astronauts on the moon – part of me was secretly hoping to find an undiscovered relic from one of the wagon trains I knew had crossed here. The return to my pioneer fantasy and my sense of relationship with the timeless story of humanity striking out in new directions, willing to endure hardship in the process, was deeper than ever in me. My move to California had been the last straw for most of my friendships in New Jersey. Anyone who had been holding out hope that I might eventually come to my senses became convinced that I truly was crazy.

Now, crossing one of the most extreme expanses on Earth, carrying only a small pack and a bottle of water, I knew that, without a doubt, the best moments of my life had been lived outside and beyond other people's ideas of what I should do. I was no longer concerned about being considered crazy. Safe, I now knew, was someone else's idea of a life, not mine.

Chisels and Wands

I walked slowly up the stairs to the kitchen where Roger was busy tossing a salad and heating soup for our lunch. As I placed plates, forks and knives on the table, I tried to work out in my head what I was going to say to Roger.

A month before, a friend had given my book proposal to an agent she knew in New York. Unbelievably to me, the agent, BG Dilworth, had called me the next day, saying he loved what I had written and wanted to represent me and show *Hannah's Gift* to publishers. The two of us worked together to refine the content of the proposal, and half an hour ago he had called to tell me he was going to send the proposal by messenger to the publishers tomorrow. He thought I should come to New York immediately in order to meet face-to-face with editors who expressed an interest in making an offer.

The whole of my life had rushed through me in the brief pause before my response. I had only $700 left in my bank account, the final remnants of my divorce settlement with Claude. I had no job, no other source of income, and in two weeks my kids were scheduled to spend the whole summer with me. And yet I also knew that I needed to go to New York. Not only did I trust BG's judgment and experience as an agent, every bone in my body wanted to go.

I felt as if I were riding on the front crest of a wave that had been building since the day I decided to leave my marriage, a movement of life energy that seemed to accelerate once I had committed to writing the book. I trusted this sense I had that I was living in the centre of my life. I felt no regrets, no matter what was about to happen. Every penny I spent in the past year and a half had been consciously spent, and every decision had been thoughtfully made. The sense that I needed to go to New York was not something I could explain rationally; it simply felt like the right next thing, arising out of the same assurance I felt that *Hannah's Gift* had a home somewhere, and the publisher it belonged to would know it.

Minutes before, I had told BG I would be there, and after hanging up, had called a travel agent and booked the cheapest last-minute flight I could find, $400 round-trip from San Francisco to New York with a one-stop layover in Chicago. Now, seated next to Roger at the kitchen table, I took a deep breath and let the story pour out.

Roger's eyes widened, and his mouth gaped open. 'Are you crazy? You only have $300 left,' he said.

Looking at him, I knew that any other time in my life I might have waffled, thought about cancelling the ticket, changed my mind. But instead I felt insulated from his anxiety. I heard his words, knowing that everything he was saying was true while also knowing that other, more important things were also true. Rather than feeling impulsive and irresponsible, I felt sure I was doing the only thing I could do.

My life, my work now was all about chisels and wands – I would do what I could, putting the words on the page, getting the proposal to BG, and flying to New York. The rest, whatever magic and grace that might happen out of it, would have to be up to God.

Everything and Nothing the Same

I was shaking as I picked up the phone to make the call. Holding the receiver close to my ear, I listened to the ring over the sounds of the busy airport around me. A man on the pay phone next to me was arguing with someone. Every 30 seconds, another airline gate attendant made a boarding announcement on the loud speaker. I barely heard any of it.

Listening to the ring of the phone in my one ear and the airline boarding announcements in the other, I felt strangely lucky, a bit giddy, reckless and wild. A few minutes before, I had called Roger to let him know I was about to board my flight to San Francisco and to tell him that, although I had no way of knowing yet whether *Hannah's Gift* was going to be published, the five meetings I'd had with publishers had gone well. Roger had sounded breathless when he answered. 'Call your agent immediately. You have an offer on your book,' he said.

Closing my eyes, I willed BG to pick up the phone. When I heard the click of the receiver and then his voice, I let out an audible sigh of relief.

'BG, it's me, Maria,' I said, my heart pounding so loud in my ear, I was afraid I might not hear his response.

'Are you sitting down?' BG asked, the excitement in his voice rising. 'Bantam has made a pre-emptive offer of $250,000.'

I felt like fainting as my awareness floated out of my body and inside it at the same time. I had been saying 'yes' to my life all these months, trusting that I was doing what my life needed me to do, following my heart in moving to California, and writing my first book. And my life, in this single moment, had turned and said 'yes' back to me.

Rings and Roses

It was the perfect first day of the rest of our lives. The sky was clear and covered with stars as country western tunes, played by The Belmont Boys, floated over the bay, and Roger and I danced in each other's arms. Twirling, I caught a glimpse of my parents holding each other close, while Will, Margaret and Madelaine smiled at everyone and dug deeper into huge pieces of chocolate wedding cake.

The most impossible dreams had finally come true. Earlier in the day, Roger and I had been married on the Bay of San Francisco by one of our best friends, Palden, a Tibetan lama, under a canopy of ribbons and flowers. I had followed my girls and Will down the aisle, wearing a long, black designer gown, and exchanged vows of love and commitment with the man I adored in front of his mother, my parents, brother and sister and 30 of our closest friends.

After the ceremony, I changed into a rich, gold slip of a dress that Roger had made for me in Bali, and everyone exchanged champagne toasts and tucked into a lovely dinner that our friends Ron and Heidi, whose house we were married in, had generously provided. It was one of those occasions where everyone was smiling and no one wanted to go home. Now, glancing at the thick, gold band on my left ring finger, dancing across pink rose petals that Madelaine had sprinkled from her white wicker basket, I smiled into Roger's eyes and could think of nothing more to dream.

Once a Mother, Always a Mother

I parked my car on the shoulder of the road and began the climb up the side of the mountain, holding the package in my hand. Today, on what would have been Hannah's eleventh birthday, I had received the first galley copy of *Hannah's Gift*. Now, settling into the grass on the slope of Mount Tamalpais, overlooking the ocean, I closed my eyes and said a prayer of gratitude for this moment.

I could hardly believe the day had finally come, that my first book, the story of Hannah's life and death, was about to come into the world. Opening my eyes, I carefully pulled the strip along the edge of the package, and pulled the book out. As soon as I saw the image of Hannah's red patent leather shoes on the pure, white cover, I started to cry. Tears streaming down my cheeks, I lay down in the grass and began reading the words that, for months, had poured out of my heart. I felt as if I might explode with pride and amazement, seeing them as I had written them, for the first time, in print, on the page.

My greatest fear, after Hannah's death, had been that she would be forgotten, that her place in my heart would disappear, erode away with the passing of grief and time. But now, as I read, I began to feel Hannah's presence, a pulsating energy inside my body, a rush of cellular human connection between her and an animal mother-love in me. I realized then, that Hannah would not only continue to be alive in the pages of this book, she would be alive forever in my bones. And knowing that, I could release her story, like a little paper boat of hope, into the river of the world.

Summer in Cornwall

The wooden door of the English cottage swung open as Will and his two new mates, twin boys who lived across the path, came in. Dumping their cricket bats and shoes in a pile on the floor, the three boys, laughing and jostling each other, ran upstairs. Smiling, I finished washing the breakfast dishes, and then glanced out the window to check on Margaret and Madelaine who were playing Barbie dolls in the garden.

Roger, the kids, and I had arranged to spend a month in the south of England, in Golant, a small fishing village in Cornwall. After only a week, it already felt like home. Our friends Brian and Deirdre, who had generously offered us the use of their cottage, helped us settle in and had already taken us for several sailing excursions on the river. Will had quickly made friends with the boys next door, and now went rowing with them every morning in sleek, narrow boats. As a family, we had gone sightseeing and had explored the neighbouring villages, but mostly we had settled into the simplicity of life on the river. Now, even the girls felt comfortable skipping down the hill every afternoon to the pub in town to buy ice cream and bags of crisps.

Wiping my hands dry on a linen towel, I opened the door to the stone terrace that stretched across the length of the house, with breathtaking views of the river Fowey below. Roger, who was sitting in a patch of morning sun, reading a book, looked up and smiled. I crossed to him and gave him a kiss. Standing at the edge of the terrace, I inhaled the cool misty air blowing from the south-west, and watched the movement of the river across the landscape.

The river was the life-giving force of this place. Fed by the ocean's tide, it moved slowly, first in one direction, then the other, filling and then draining down to the mud each day. The girls and I loved walking across it once the water had receded, feeling the soft, brown muck squish between our toes, and touching the bottoms of the boats tied to buoys, tipped on their sides, waiting patiently for the river to return.

Listening to the excited voices of the boys upstairs, wafting out of an open window, and the girls' quieter murmur rising from the garden, I felt a sense of peace for the way that Will, Margaret, Madelaine and I, along with Roger, were creating a sense of family and home in a larger, less foreign world.

Start Walking

I was in the middle of the strangest dream. A vast sea of faces was turned towards me, each one looking at me with fearful, uncertain eyes. I had a sense that they were the undead – souls that had not yet fully crossed over – and they wanted me to help. Before I could do anything, though, the phone rang, waking me up.

I glanced at the clock before swinging my legs over the side of the bed. It was early, just after 7 am. Roger, his eye-shade on and earplugs in, was still sleeping soundly next to me. The phone was ringing insistently, so I jumped up quickly and answered it. Our friend, Jeremiah, was breathless on the other end.

'I know you guys don't have a television,' he said, his voice cracking as if he was crying. 'You'll never believe what's just happened. The east coast is under attack! Passenger planes have just crashed into the Pentagon and the World Trade Center.'

For a split second, I thought I must be dreaming as I struggled to wrap my mind around what Jeremiah had just said.

But the racing of my heart and the breathlessness I now felt couldn't be anything but real.

'Oh my God, my kids are there,' I cried out. 'I have to get off the phone and call someone,' I said, hanging up.

Roger, hearing my shout, sat up, disoriented. 'What's wrong?' he said.

I told him what Jeremiah had said as I frantically dialled the principal's office at the girls' school. The secretary answered on my first ring, and assured me that the children were safe and would not be released until their continued safety was assured. I told her to call me if there was any change, and then threw on some clothes and told Roger I was going next door, to our friends' house to see what was happening on television.

All that day, as the images of the Pentagon and World Trade Center smouldered in front of my eyes, I knew only one thing. I had once believed that I could live across the country from my kids, but I believed something very different now. I had to return to them, to the east coast. If they needed me or I needed them, I wanted to live close enough to simply start walking.

Christmas Wish

Roger and I were sitting on the couch in the apartment in New York City, with Will, Margaret and Madelaine squished in between us. The tiny Christmas tree we had purchased from the street vendor stood in one corner of the room, festooned with white lights and white paper snowflakes the kids had cut out, and topped with a tin foil star.

'I have a Christmas surprise for you guys,' I said, so excited about telling them, it was all I could do to keep from blurting it out.

'What, what, what?' the three of them shouted.

'Roger and I are moving,' I said, drawing the suspense out as long as I could, 'We're buying a house, right here, in New York.' I was grinning, anticipating their delight. Instead, the three of them were silent, looking at each other, and then Roger and me.

'Do you mean we won't be living in California anymore?' Will asked quietly. Then, he quickly added, 'It's not that we're not excited about you living closer to Dad's, it's just that we really liked it there.'

I was stunned, truly stunned. I had spent weeks, since September 11, playing the scene over and over in my mind, imagining all three kids crying with happiness and relief, knowing Roger and I would now be living just down the road. Now, I realized it was my guilt as a mother that had staged the imagined scene. The truth was, while it hadn't been easy for any of us to be living so far apart, it hadn't been as difficult as I had believed either.

'It *will* be fun to live closer to each other, Mom,' Margaret said finally, giving me a hug.

'Yeah,' Will said, smiling now. 'I have to admit, I was hoping you'd stay in California for at least a couple more years. The legal driving age there is 16, and here in New Jersey it's a year later. I was really looking forward to having my licence before all of my friends.'

Madelaine, who had been silent until now, leaned over and gave me a kiss. 'It's okay that you're moving to New York, Mommy,' she said. 'Besides, you always did tell us, "Momma always comes back."'

Tough Love

I pulled my car into Claude's driveway, and checked the clock. I was five minutes early. I shut off the engine, unbuckled my seatbelt and opened the door. Approaching the house, I realized some part of me still felt as if I lived there, even though it had been more than five years since the divorce. So many of my memories had been made in this place, especially my memories of Hannah, who, $8\frac{1}{2}$ years later, sometimes seemed like a good idea I once had, rather than the little girl I would do anything for. She was here, along with traces of the woman I once was, imbued on every surface in the house, every brick in the sidewalk and every blade of grass on the lawn.

Peeking through the window into the entry hall, I rang the front doorbell. I could see the gold-framed mirror and welcome sign in the same place I'd hung them when we had first moved in. Although Claude had not allowed me inside since our divorce was final, I knew that some things had changed. From the kids, I knew that there was now a computer in the living room, and the nursery/playroom had been converted to a bedroom for the au pair.

Margaret came running to the door and opened it. 'Hi Mom!' she said, throwing her arms around me. 'We're just finishing packing our stuff. We'll be right out.'

'Okay, no hurry,' I said, smiling. 'I'll wait.'

Returning to the car, I leaned back in the front seat. Just then, I heard a loud roar, as Claude, pushing the lawnmower, came around the corner of the house. I smiled and felt my heart do a somersault. I still felt a deep affection for him, as impossible as it might seem. More than anything, I wanted to be able to jump out of the car, run up to him and say hello. I could even imagine him shutting the lawnmower off for a moment so we could have a conversation, catch up on each other's lives, while I waited for the kids.

But none of this was possible, and I knew it. Claude still hadn't spoken a single word to me, on the phone or in person, for more than five years, refusing even to look at me when we crossed paths. For a long time, I had implored him, via e-mail and letter, to consider how harmful this was for our kids. But I had gradually understood that the more I pushed to engage him, the more I was playing into the damaging dynamics between us. I began to suspect that his silence was an attempt to freeze things between us in order to keep them, like the house, forever what they were.

But I was no longer who I was, although some traces still remained. Almost 40 years old now, my sense of self was less dependent on the actions and beliefs of others. I had turned a corner somewhere along the line, and now knew that my life was all about permission – permission to be imperfect, to make mistakes, to be afraid. And in giving myself permission to be and experience all these things, I was also able to grant the same permission to those I loved. For me, life was no longer about being 'good'; it was about being true.

Watching Claude now, pushing the lawnmower back and forth across the front yard, his brow creased in concentration – or perhaps in an effort to ignore me – I knew I could not change how he chose to behave. But I *could* choose how to deal with it. Rather than needing to embarrass him, shame him or make him wrong, I chose to see him as a human being, like me: imperfect, struggling and learning. And seeing that, I also chose to continue to love and respect him for what we had once shared together, for being the father of the children we both loved. While I would never give up hope that things might eventually ease between us, I could be at peace with the way it was, knowing now that loving fully *really does* mean letting go.

Log Cabin

I cleared the paper-plate puppets off the picnic table on the back porch, and then called to the girls who were building a tepee out of branches they had dragged from the woods into the back yard.

'It's time to get ready for your art lesson,' I said.

'Okay, Mom, we're coming,' they called back.

It was summer, and we were now living in New York, in a log cabin, perched on the shoulder of a mountain just outside Woodstock. Bare, stripped logs, each once a tree, had been stacked and fitted together to make our home. A huge stone fireplace and woodstove stood in the living room, and two long porches stretched along the front and back of the house. Will and the girls spent their weekends and summers roaming the woods, collecting tiny newts and building forts. Sometimes the four of us pulled Roger away from his writing studio, and we would all walk down the hill to visit with neighbours or wade and fish in the stream.

Now, standing on the dirt road at the end of our drive, wearing faded Levi's, one of my Dad's old workshirts, and a pair of lapis earrings from Morocco, my hair pulled back into a pony tail, I watched the girls skipping down the hill towards Ted, our friend and neighbour, who was a retired film-maker and part-time artist. Days before, Margaret had spotted him painting a picture on an easel in his front yard and boldly asked him to give her and Madelaine art lessons. Smiling, he had agreed.

Watching the girls now, holding Ted's hands, waving to me as they disappeared around the bend, I suddenly felt over-whelmed by a sense of déjà vu. I realized then, in that moment, that my life had finally come full circle from the day I had walked to the end of the dirt road at the retreat centre and slid my postcards into the mailbox. I was finally the woman I had always believed I could be, a wife and mother, fully in her life, watching her daughters fully in theirs.

My life now felt as incomplete and perfect as a mother's day when everyone is safe and asleep but there is still a load of laundry in the dryer as she climbs into bed. I was at peace with the gap between who I was and what I knew, and will-ing to accept that while I knew a great many things, I was still so few of them. But I also had no need right now to pre-tend that I was a part-time mom wishing I were a full-time one. Although, in my heart, I fully expected that one day I would return to being a mother full-time, for now I loved that the flexibility I had as a writer, combined with our cus-tody arrangement, afforded me space and solitude in which to work during the school year when the kids lived with Claude, and then allowed me to give Will, Margaret and Madelaine my full attention when I was with them.

And while Roger's love for me and for my children was a part of the peace I now experienced, I was no longer interested in having a perfect life or a perfect marriage. I now understood that the struggles and challenges of relationship are an inherent part of the package, and that the heart of a good marriage is the love that sustains it and that allows us, individually and separately, to grow. Roger's darkness and my own were things I was still learning to fall in love with, and more and more I was learning to trust many of the things it had to teach me.

While I was still certain I had made the right decision in divorcing Claude, I knew that I might never know for sure whether I had done the right thing in giving him primary custody of our children. Everything looks different when we turn around and see all those abandoned campsites, those people we once were. But what I did trust, without question, as I turned and strolled back to the cabin, was that what I had said to Will alongside that campfire in Kansas more than four years before, was still true: who I was and what I knew was constantly changing, but the love I felt for my children, for Roger, and even for Claude, was solid, unwavering. It was the best of who I was.

Epilogue

La Mère (the Mother), La Mer (the Sea)

AS I WRITE THESE WORDS, THE EPILOGUE OF THIS BOOK, IT IS important to me that you, the reader, know that Roger and I, between the two of us, now own two places: his, a sweet one-bedroom in the West Village of Manhattan, and mine, a con-dominium across the river from the apartment where I lived the first year after my divorce. Taking the ferry back and forth, we live our lives separately and together. But more importantly, I have finally returned to my rightful place by my kids and the sea.

Not long ago, as Roger and I left a theatre in New York City, I received a phone call from Madelaine, who is now eight years old. As I stood in the middle of a busy sidewalk in Manhattan, my cell phone pressed against my ear, listening to her play a piano piece she intended to perform at her recital, the bittersweetness of the moment was not lost on me. I have given up more than I ever imagined I would have to give in order to live this life that I know, without a doubt, is mine. There are many days when my heart still aches to be more with my kids, but I also know and trust that I am close to and still dis-covering my changes.

And each morning as I sit on my terrace, sipping my cof-fee and gazing out at the ocean, I feel blessed to be reminded that every river, no matter its twists and bends, always returns to the sea. **"**

Note: the quotation marks positioned around the story are intentional, an offering to the way all our stories are simply one version of what happened, no better or worse, truer or less true than anyone else's memory or perspective.

Acknowledgements

Every life owes a debt of gratitude to those who either willingly or unwittingly offered themselves to it. Mine is no different. To Roger Housden, my beloved husband, to Will, Hannah, Margaret and Madelaine, my cherished children, and to countless friends, teachers, family members and guides, my faith is stronger and my heart softer because of your presence in my life and I am grateful.

About the Author

MARIA HOUSDEN, SINCE THE AGE OF 12, DREAMED OF WRITING a book. Instead, after graduating from university, she became a financial analyst, then an at-home wife and mother. Five years ago, she began writing. Her first book, *Hannah's Gift: Lessons from a Life Fully Lived*, was published in 2001 and has become an international bestseller, translated into more than 15 foreign languages. Maria is now an author and lecturer, and lives with her husband Roger in New York and New Jersey.

Readers' responses can be e-mailed to unravelled@juno.com.

Also by Maria Housden

Hannah's Gift

Lessons from a Life Fully Lived

DURING THE LAST YEAR OF HER SHORT LIFE, MARIA HOUSDEN'S three-year-old daughter Hannah was fearless in the way she faced death – and irrepressibly joyful in the way she approached living. The little girl who wore her favourite red shoes into the operating theatre changed the life of everyone who came into contact with her.

In a lyrically told narrative, both moving and unforgettable, Housden recounts Hannah's battle with cancer in simple, straightforward language that transcends grief and fear to become a celebration. A remarkable story, remarkably told, it will bring comfort to anyone touched by loss, and renewed faith in the power of love.

'A heartbreaking and heartwarming tale of a fearless little girl.' *People Magazine*

'Hannah has a philosophy on life that is unique and tears the heart apart.' *The Bookseller*

S P E C I A L   O F F E R

Order these selected Thorsons and Element titles direct from the publisher and receive £1 off each title! Visit www.thorsonselement.com for additional special offers.

Free post and packaging for UK delivery (overseas and Ireland, £2.00 per book).

Hannah's Gift Maria Housden (0007155670)	£6.99 retail – £1 = £5.99
The Gift Mia Dolan (0007154518)	£6.99 retail – £1 = £5.99
Dave Pelzer's Life Lessons Dave Pelzer (0007146914)	£4.99 retail – £1 = £3.99
Help Yourself Dave Pelzer (000711480X)	£6.99 retail – £1 = £5.99

Place your order by post, phone, fax, or email, listed below. Be certain to quote reference code **713Q** to take advantage of this special offer.

Mail Order Dept. (REF: **713Q**)
HarperCollins*Publishers*
Westerhill Road
Bishopbriggs G64 2QT

Email: customerservices@harpercollins.co.uk
Phone: 0870 787 1724
Fax: 0870 787 1725

Credit cards and cheques are accepted. Do not send cash. Prices shown above were correct at time of press. Prices and availability are subject to change without notice.

BLOCK CAPITALS PLEASE

Name of cardholder _____
Address of cardholder _____
_____
_____

Postcode _____

Delivery address (if different)
_____
_____
_____

Postcode _____

I've enclosed a cheque for £_____, made payable to HarperCollins*Publishers*, or please charge my Visa/MasterCard/Switch (circle as appropriate)

Card Number: _____

Expires: __/__   Issue No: __/__   Start Date: __/__
Switch cards need an issue number or start date validation.

Signature:_____

thorsons
element

Make
www.thorsonselement.com
your online sanctuary

Get online information, inspiration and
guidance to help you on the path to physical
and spiritual well-being. Drawing on the integrity
and vision of our authors and titles, and with
health advice, articles, astrology, tarot, a
meditation zone, author interviews and events
listings, www.thorsonselement.com is a great
alternative to help create space and peace
in our lives.

So if you've always wondered about practising
yoga, following an allergy-free diet, using the
tarot or getting a life coach, we can point you
in the right direction.